# Captured

# Comprehensive

### AND

# Defined

Copywrite 2012

by *William Thompson Jr.*

**PUBLISHED BY**

Write Everlasting Tips,
Publishing company

ISBN-0-978-9755994-6-1

Unless otherwise indicated,
all Scripture quotations are from the
King James Version of the Bible.

Printed in the United States of America

To contact the author, write
W E T Publishing Co.
7525 Arbor Hill Dr.
Fort Worth, Texas 76120

All rights reserved. Written permission must
be secured from the publisher to use or reproduce
any part of this book, except for brief quotations
embodied in church related publications,
critical review or articles.

# Contents

Dedication..................................IV
About The Author........................V
Introduction...............................VII

1. Undertanding Assignments................17
2. The Purpose of Integrity....................37
3. On The Premise of The Blood............55
4. Power of Recognition........................79
5. Guilty Justice.....................................91
6. Reprobate Mind...............................105
7. Powerful Preaching..........................123
8. Fire..................................................141
9. Right Now.......................................163

Conclusion..
    My Final Say On The Matter...179

# Dedication

*To: my Lord and Savior, and to the the awaiting Body of Christ;*

I write the things given to me with sincere Love for enlightenment of the placed platform of Faith to enable others to step up to walk closer with God, so that they might be elevated in their understandng for the benefit of sharing and preparing others for the eminate return of our Lord...............

My family; the object of all my affection and Love; Mrs. Sharon Thompson, Antonio, Miss Misty, Aaron, & William III.......... Thank you for your love and support

*From deeply within me; I Levy this work upon you..............*

# About The Author

## William (Bill) Thompson Jr.

Has been in the ministry of preaching the gospel since Feb. 7, 1982, and has engaged in studies and training of the bible. He has been in the church all of his natural life and has the experience of a true churchman that lends the passion for which he ministers the gospel of God. He is an ordained ministering elder of the Church since June 1998.

He attended the Fort Worth Independant School District and graduated from P. L. Dunbar Sr. High, class of 79'. He attended Tarrant County Junior College, Dallas Theological Seminary, and Vogue Beauty College.

His uncle; the late Apostle Russell Thompson, laid hands on him at the age of 11, from that point on he knew that there was more for him in the Lord. He is a talented instrumentalist, and has composed many songs. Pastor Thompson has crossed the lines of denominational influences as a friend and brother, enabling himself to become identified as a child of God and not Just a Baptist, a Methodist, a Pentecostal, or as just another member of the Church Of God In Christ!

He is known and respected as a "True Prophet" of God. Pastor Thompson has been married to Sharon Renee for 28 years and is the father of four children.

# Thank

𝔚rite 𝔈verlasting 𝔗ips 𝔓ublishing 𝔗o., will faithfully continue the Assignment of penning the revealed truths from the Lord, publishing the Excellence of God's Word..........

Other Available Topics @ Google, Amazon.com Hidden N' The Light, Once Bitten ForEver, Shepherd Wars & Sheep Attacks, Just Let Jesus Do It For You, Word Up, It's Got To Come Out Of Your Mouth........ More to come; and Music By Apostle/Prophet WilliamThompson Jr

# Introduction

  I am often quoted, read and even heard speaking being one desiring the ultimate optimum effectiveness of our Christian faith! I may appear to be rather high-strung at times, seeking entryways into the thought processes of the minds of the people that hear me speaking, or to those who have read or may soon read my Christian materials; wanting them to know the Lord. But, even though my desire is great; people will have to receive the Lord on their own recognance and faith.

  Many leaders have taken upon themselves to redefine Christ and Christianity, of which I myself will forever refuse to do so. They have moved beyond the call just to introduce the Lord and savior Jesus Christ to the people thinking it best and even feeling compelled to deminish and even sometimes to demolish any preconceived ideas about Christ that the people may already have who come into their churches, all across the country and around the world.

It is not always the direct intent of those who stand in called out representation of Christ, to take it upon themselves to give a validated definition to the person of Christ; as Christ speaks for Himself beyond human comprehension!

If we don't watchfully maintain our faithfulness to the word of God in total assurance of our hope in God through the power of the blood, we may soon find that we have become the scientific myth-busters of faith against the carnal stance of secular humanist who have already scientifically ruled out the written biblical truth in Christ as factual.

Posturing ourselves on the defensive can lead us unintentionally into areas of scientific evaluations to lend explanations of our positions in Christ, against the established biblically based explanations of our faith. The Scientific society have a way of pushing believers to fight against negative oppositions of faith, using their rules of science in the teaching sessions in our bible schools and across the pulpit on any Sunday morning.

Having faith in the teaching preachers, and evangelist of the faith that we are to become reliant upon, we are dealing with receiving as the ultimate purpose for listening to them. It is the responsibility of every believer not to take the wrong thing home in the spirit of our minds and in our hearts as if we had been on a shopping spree, as there is no return or a refund; you could find yourself stuck in lying deception for the rest of your life! God cannot be boxed into any one single set of ideas or methods outside of the truth in the written word of God in the Holy bible.

There is but one Lord; we are all determined to introduce to the people which defines our purpose as ministers, in doing so. Those of us who handle the same infallible word of God, the "King James Bible;" our inner-drive is to take people beyond just hearing and reading the word of God to make decisions themselves to receive the Lord and to personally seek His face for a revelation of truth that will be defining of who the Lord is!

God; in His own infinate wisdom, has already determined that if any man, woman, boy or girl decide that they really want to know the Lord Jesus in the fullness of His power, and in the pardening of sins, that if they would seek the Lord with their whole heart, they would find Him and be found of Him!

**Received, Not Perceived!**

To perceive/receive; in either case scenario, the ability to do so lies within the competent scope of reasoning in the thought process of every individual. But, there are contrasting differences between the two. While the one will require the mental capacity (space or the ability to contain) to do so, the other requires the mental capability (intellectual readiness of mental skills) to accomplish the desired performance of the mind.

As it relates to receiving the Lord, the problem often lies within the fact that an individual may be closed-minded to the idea of needing the help of the Lord in the first place. Many very rich and financially wealthy people fall prey to the desire to reject the hand of God, believing that they have everything that they need already within their own means, financially. Though they are often deceived, they believe that if money can't do it; it can't or it shouldn't even be done!

Ignorant of needing to open up to the Lord, in an effort to allow Him space to enter our lives; as we open up for the Lord, simultaneously we are opening the escape to exit from the darkened dungeons of inward torment. We enable ourselves to remain locked away from the freedom of our own deliverance while we struggle to open the door for the Lord to enter in.

God knows the weaklings that we are, so He would never require us to do something that would be totally impossible for us to do. He loves us much greater than that!

Opening up to receive the Lord is not the problem to be concerned with at all, as it is the simplest thing to do. Making up our minds to go ahead and do it is usually the problem. The sweet winds of change are blowing through our atmosphere, but, we must open the windows of our minds and the doors of our hearts before we will ever be able to breathe in the refreshing alterations of mental and spiritual renewal.

Far too many people; desiring to receive more of the Lord, are disadvantaged to increase in the knowledgeable understanding of the Lord for the simple reason of the fact that their lack of faith has rendered their capacity to spiritually maintain the greater things of the Lord; too small! That, that they have already received of the Lord is spilling out and running all over their plates unintentionally. They have not yet learned to handle what they already have.

Spiritually; they are walking on springs that have not yet even matured to become stabled legs causing them to vacillate back and forth between truth and lies; living and dying; between that that is holy and what is truly sinful; thus thay have no fortifide definitions to stand on. The platforms of deception are set to be accepted as the truth.

They seek to understand before they are even awarded the opportunities to receive, and they often never come to the point of being able to totally comprehend spiritually what they have received, or why it is that they have never received anything from the Lord. This same behavior has also been applied to receiving the Lord Jesus; as savior and deliverer.

While most who stand to declare the mystery of the gospel of God might have read the second chapter of Genesis, not all have understood the purpose for the instructions that were given to Adam in the garden, concerning the trees that were in the midst of the garden.

Satan has been at work to obscure the understanding of mankind from the beginning of time even up to this present generation. Since from the beginning of time, God; has always been revealed through inner-personal relationships, as of which in these latter times it requires prayerful communication with God.

We have to talk to God in accordance to His word in an effort to know the things of God without the possibilities of any human error. God and Adam spoke person to person and mouth to mouth in the garden until they were separated as result of sin in the garden.

Adam and Eve knew everything that God knew about everything that had been created. All they knew from the beginning was God indeed; God's warning to them was solely for the purpose of protecting them from the schemes of the enemy that had not even as of yet been introduced to the atmospheric scope of humanity.

I'd like very much to encourage your mind to understand that Adam and Eve woke up to God in their mornings; they did not have to seek for Him, or to remain prayerful in an effort to remain in touch with Him! The connecting bind as we would understand it today between man and God was so, at each waking moment of the day, all the day long around the clock.

## Introduction

When you know God; you have come to know it all, even though it has not all been revealed to you, and it very well may never be totally released into the scope of your own reasoning. God doesn't need you to help! He is complete and entire in His total consistency; there is not one iota, or even a jot or tittle of any information that God does not know! What God needs most of us is to simply receive Him in total obedience of faith.

From the very point and entrance of sin into the world, humanity developed the anxiety to question God rather than to patiently receive Him. Mankind had now begun to acquire knowledge of the things that had been previously unknown to them. Man never knew that there would be alternative opinions relative to the things that had been created.

People have been deceived into believing that they have learned better ways of living alternatively to God's ways; they have actually discovered swifter avenues of dying that lead us down the pathways of death. Sense we have learned how to die; as mankind, it seems now that we are dying more rapidly by the day. Strategies of warfare showed us even greater methods of sending multiples of people to the grave all at once. All of this we have leaned, simply because knowing God was never enough!

The sadistic genes of Satan are intertwined with man which developed the appetite to dissect every eternal fiber of God's being, if it were possible. It is not that man really wants to intimately know God; man has been infected with wanting to know what makes God who and what He is; men really want to know all about God without ever being personally acquainted with God.

Even from the the Tower of Babel in Genesis 11th chapter; mankind developed the sadistic mad and evil rage to obtain an internal insight to god having no reverential esteem to worship Him as God; as He is.

God wants us to believe firstly, which will enable us to know the things of God that we desire to know. Mankind and Satan, have a tendency to use the acquisition of knowledge to destroy the very basic necessity for having faith in God. This is a tragedy because there are things about God that knowledge doesn't even have the capacity to know or to comprehend.

God is never against the acquisition of knowledge. Being smart doesn't excite God at all because smart is what God made us! Albert Einstein was not even close to being as smart as Adam! Often times being smart here in the earth is relative to being the first individual to acquire the knowledge. If such should be the true definition here in the earth, it is for sure that Adam got here first!

People think that they are being intelligent when saying; "if God will answer me first, I will give Him a try!" People believe that they have to intellectually perceive God before they can trust in Him, and seek Him for change.

The stupidity of thinking that God can be manipulated by way of human intelligence pushes mankind into thinking that God need us to make it. While God did make mankind only after the fall of Lucifer; man was made out of the love of God's own heart according to His will, in His own likeness and in His own image; after God's own desire, but not out of any need!

### Driven to Miss God!

Man has long since before now, driven past go! People are so far gone with wanting to be in control that they have consistently pushed right pass the presence of the Lord. It appears that man has a need to drive right pass the filling station, though we may be consistently running on an empty tank. We're out of Gas! And we are in need of changing the oil! The very service that we are in need of receiving, often we are set on avoiding it.

We are often so driven that we don't even realize when we have overrun the exit of self to enter the very presence of the Lord which is usually our needed destination. In this book it is my endeavor to enable you to redirect your thinking on some areas of acquired thought provoking information which will in turn help you to get on the right side of the right road to your intended destination; which is God indeed, whereas you will never miss the entrance or the exit.

Follow me throughout the topical dialogues of this book, line by line; looking up as you drive by, being sure not to miss any of the onramps to higher thinking and comprehensive understanding. Extend the mental reach upwards towards God determining to touch God, and you will never miss Him.

It has been my pleasure to pen' such captured understanding of the topics relative to each chapter. In my own heart I am impressed to believe that people need a more comprehensive definition to many of the given categories for suggested biblical understanding and instruction, for which it has been rather amplified in its compiled structure, by this author.

Thanks for taking the time to explore the data written to the direct interest of those who are in the body of The Christ.

Much Love to you, and may the Lord God bless you real good……………………….

# Chapter One

# UNDERSTANDING ASSIGNMENTS

---

*The steps of a good man are ordered by the Lord; and he delighteth in his way.* **Psalms 37:23**

## Out of Order

Often while writing, and publishing the literary works of books, magazine and Newspaper articles, etc...; the type generated voice tones of the writers are misinterpreted and given harsh descriptions of negative undertones. Upon reading what has been penned, something seems to trigger in the minds of the critical reviewers suggesting that they could have indeed said it better than the writer, or at least that the writer could have, or should have said it much more differently?

Disregarding the fact that the writer intended to say it just the way that they did; It is easy for those that read to cite all of the missing statements and comments, misspelled words and even the omitted basic elementary punctuations, or maybe even what they may feel should be the more defining substancial information crucial for letting the reader into the mind of the writer; from the published literary works.

Those who don't do and have never ever done anything of their own always seem to believe that they can teach those that do, lessons on getting it done. Amazingly, those who criticize the constructive achievements of others, they usually never creatively mobilize the transmissive idealistic thinking in their own minds in discipline to write! It is not that they are always jealous of the accomplishments of others, they just think that they have better skills, even though they don't have any literary accomplishments of their own! They've Done Nothing!

Although reading and writing go together like a

hand and an arm, knowing the difference between the two necessary members, plays the part of the adjoining wrist to make both parts functional to each other which would be the conjoined power in the connection.

Just because an individual may be an advid reader, that doesn't also make them to be a prolific writer automatically. Any reader may in fact know what to look for when reading books or literary works, but knowing how to place it there when writing can be a bit incredulous, as one has to know the skill of separating fact from fiction, feelings from faith, and mostly they need to know the difference between man and God; which is alarmingly paramount!

Good grammatical skills don't produce great Christian writers, either! So much more is involved in being the spirit led writer; whereas all of the spiritual pistons should be firing to successfully enable the subject data to rest on the pages of the written material. Critiques, without knowing it most times, have the tendency to over value the power of their own word placement skills, being able to cite when word usage is out of contextual order.

What actually makes being opinionated a dangerous thing, is that the formed opinions are irreversably damaging and based on thinking over and against the establishment of others findings, personalities, and/or the compiled statements of other author's finished works of factual findings. It's only their thoughts on any particular matter! Critics rely upon their ability to dissuade or to persuade the thinking capacity of others.

The greater derivation of corporate power struggles stems from what seems to be the denial to allow others to intellectualize the higher elevated corporate knowledge, tantamount in comparison to that of the upper level management personnel. Everything that an individual thinks in their own mind will not always be attainable to them.

Some people feel that they can swim the ocean from the United States to the coast of Africa; but they are gravely being mentally misinformed. There are times when the condition of the water is too tumultuous, that some certain fish even swim away to find calmer waters! Swimming from coast to coast is not hinged upon skill as a good swimmer; water temperament and the aquatic predators that inhabit the water are gravely to be taken into consideration, relative to the precarious woeful conditions they create!

Overinflated egotistical self confidence often create situations that are forever impossible, for the sake of the inability to think on every level that makes for bringing an idea into a reality. No matter how smart you might be, your one mind does not make up the necessary pieces to create a corporation all by itself! Too many people have not even considered the fact that there are several people employed with the same company of employment as they are themselves for a reason.

God never intended for mankind to live on any other planet of the cosmos other than the earth! Just because it has become possible for man to go to the moon, doesn't make it a reality to go there and stay permanently! It is egotistical and arrogant to think of such as being humanly possible!

Many are subject to misread written messages, as many people are prone to be super-sensitive and highly defensive in relation to direct messages that speak to their own misguided behavior. When out of order, people approach reading materials from the initialized standpoint that their purpose for reading was not necessarily to connect with the writer's message. So often the only motivational drive that intrigues the reader to engage a literary work is recreational entertainment.

Many books that adorn the bookshelves of stores, libraries, offices and etc.; are loaded with information that have missed the intellectual process of reasoning in the minds of readers, simply for the misdiagnosis to the meaningful message of the writer's assignment relative to the title on the book cover. For the sake of the seriousness of the reading material that was never intended for the purpose of entertainment, the reading funny-bone could not be tickled.

Take into consideration that many of these similar readers in personality, take to the pages of the written word of God, on a quest for literary intrigue, for the purpose of deflating the purported authenticity in the bible. They think that they need to disprove that the bible is a necessary tool for us in these latter generations. They crack the pages of the bible having their interpretation skills exaggerated to maximum levels, as if to be the defining authority on the thought provocation of the scripture.

I say often that there is too much interpretation and not enough revelation among those of us who are reading the word of God on a daily basis; and here's why: Interpretation tells others and attemps at telling God what we think that He is saying to us and what it is that we prefer to believe!

However, Revelation; in truthful retrospection, is God telling us exactly what He is saying to us through the aid of the Holy Spirit, and it subscribes to us what we are to believe relative to our acquisitions of faith in God. I have said it before but I'm going to say it again, we don't know what God is saying to us unless He tells us first!

## Assignment, or Designation?

Critical examiners have caused such an enormous uproar among the people of the society and in the churches all on their own ability to dissuade the reader's cognizance to rightly comprehend what has been stated in writing. Those who are allowed to criticize literary works, they often lose the ability to feel what the writer is actually saying, whether they agree or disagree.

Never forget the fact that as readers we both think and feel what has been levied upon our minds through literary works. Whenever we put a book down after having read a chapter or two, it does not necessarily constitute the fact that the book had also been closed in our minds. We might have closed the book with our hands but our minds continue to scan the written materials which had just been imputed into our thought process. The mind continues to compute, breaking down the meaningful dialogue of the written data.

*Understanding Assignments*

I never thought that people would be able to amass a living as a professional critic or even a skilled complainer. Many critiques are never satisfied with anything that they come into contact with, as they are always preoccupied with fault finding, seeking errors. Critiques do not always intend to capture the writer's definition of speaking for the purpose of comprehending the writer's message.

Editors that are too critical, often may not rate very highly among those most respected, as they are often overboard when glancing through a literary work. They are often looking too hard to see the assignment of the writer, determined to establish what should be their eminent designation. They position themslves to designate where the writer and their written message is to be placed among the informative network of believers and unbelievers alike.

Assignment - *a task that is assigned or undertaken, a position, duty, or job for which somebody is chosen, the process of giving a value, use, task, or position to somebody or something, [law] a document such as a deed that effects a legal transfer of rights, [law] the transfer of a right in or over property to another person.*

Designation - *a name, label, or description given to something or somebody; the act or process of being named or specified. Nickname..................................*

Misdiagnosis have placed the understanding of the church's position in society in a negative light, even among the professed; tithe paying members of the local congregations. The neighboring communities are consistent of an increased influx of people who stay at home on Sunday mornings disgruntled with the activities of the local churches. Leaving the assignment of the church, they are now misinformed, believing that they are responsible for the beneficial placement of the local church in the neighborhood; community.

God's true assignment and prototype of the church is to show the world the savior, and to nurture people from all walks of life into the knowledge of the truth about Christ; He came to save us from sin. Society however, has chosen to designate the church as an entity in the community available to pick up the unwanted people, to provide for them an alternative to government assistance.

It is not possible always, for the church to put forth the strength of its God given assignment to the community for the sake of the bureaucratic designation among the more highly educated people of the society who feel that they have everything that they need. Many people come to the Lord for the purpose of having their need met, and their problems fixed! They were not always informed that the Lord has a purpose for them now being saved from sin and shame.

Many who have gotten on their feet as a result of turning to the Lord, have misinterpreted the idea of now living for the Lord among the people of the society. They have allowed others who were never in the shape of living as they were themselves, to sway their thinking. Having more lucrative careers and jobs, whereas they have better sociable status among the who's who of society and more money in their bank accounts; they have blinded the minds of the renewed soberly thinking individuals of the church.

They no longer believe that their purpose is to bring other people in to the salvation of the Lord, as much as they now believe that the Lord will change their ability to live among the society's most elite, whereas they were never able to do so before coming to the Lord to change their way of living!

They came for the prosperity of the people in the church who have learned to change their spending behavior and to alter their ethics of supporting the local churches financially. Most of the churches have abandoned crusades which benefit in introducing the people to Christ, for the more lucrative conferences that are targeted to inform the people of the churches to conduct better business habits and deal brokering............

Having sociable knowledge of the churches message of prosperity, possibly knowing that many of the churches had dropped the ball, causing some people to look for that which comes from only working hard and diligently applying knowledge to their skill, really didn't matter to the leaders of the society because the lessened position of the church now that the object of worship appear to be money, allows for a larger cushion against change for those who are determined to live contrary to the word of God.

Society says to the church; now do this instead of doing so much of that in the bible, and you can become a more acceptable entity and a formidable force among the communities. The secular leaders of the society, have said among themselves, let's reposition

*Captured; Comprehensive; & Defined*

the church to alter the purpose of its message and we will no longer be threatened with the church's assignment to the world.

It's been too simple for the society to wash out the assignment of the church among the community. The actual problem with the church lies within the fact that the leaders should be spiritual but they are secular in every manner of their expression as a leader. They talk to a judge better than they do Jesus; they are more successful at getting newspapers to see them and their churches than they are at getting the people to envision Jesus through the word of God. They stand on street corners for political issues and fundraising rallies, but they have no interest in going to the streets to compell men to come to Christ.

## The Pen Mightier Than the Sword?

> And take the helmet of salvation, and the sword of the spirit, which is the word of God.
> **Ephesians 6: 17**
>
> For the word of God is quick, and powerful, and sharper than any two-edge sword, piercing even to the dividing asunder of soul and spirit, and of the joints and marrow, and is a discerner of the thoughts and intents of the heart. **Hebrews 4: 12**

The pen is a designated instrument of choice; whereas, the sword is an assigned instrument of purpose. The sword of the spirit is the word of God; in its most accurate description it is in representation to the oracle authority, spoken by God. A very profound truth is that whatever the Lord says is right! God's; words, initializes all that represents truth, holiness, and righteousness. Everywhere; the word of God remains the same.

The establishment of the sword of God is not ever relevant to time, as it is and has always been an eternal element of truth. The eternal depths of the word of God are so far beyond any human capacity to undergird or to uproot; although mere men have maintained the desire to get underneath the word of God not being able to realize that the foundational platform, for which the word of God affirmatably rests, is God!

Many people have a drive within themselves to know the word of God without the aid of the Holy Ghost, being unbelieving of the spirit and of God; which is the present working power of the spirit of the Lord right now to teach us and to reveal the hidden manna within the word of God that we could not know otherwise; no matter how hard we try.

> But the Comforter, which is the Holy Ghost, whom the Father will send in my name, he shall teach you all things, and bring all things to your remembrance, whatsoever I have said unto you.
> **St. John 14: 26**

Mere men surrender to the pen, while they most often war against the sword (of the spirit); thus being the word of God.

Here's why: men have searched for centuries

*Captured; Comprehensive; & Defined*

and have found the word of God to be most powerful and accurate where it relates to where we stand as humanity, and through all of the scientific research and scholastic studies the truth of the infallible platform had been realized in measures too extreme to be further thought of as removing, and too eternally affixed to ever reconsider altering it to better serve the selfish agendas of mankind.

Earthbound, mere human beings; war against the even tide in the powerful earth flow of the word of God, while we struggle to comprehend how it is that such an earth targeted word is sent to the earth from heaven; while yet being heaven bound simultaneously. The word of God returns to the Father in heaven, reporting assuredly that it has accomplished that which He; the Father, Himself; had originally ordained!

We purport to understand the cycles of life here in the earth teaching in Science, Geography, Mathematical and History classes as we consistently miss the anointed circulatory movement of the spirit throughout the word of God which is the very source and the continuance of this present and all future existence of life. By the spirit of the word, and the word of the spirit, all things live and progressively flourish to reproduce after each; its own kind.

Intellectually, we seek to get deeply into the word of God, not always willing to allow the word of God to get deeply into us. It is the human drive to have command over the word of God whereas initially the word of God commanded us to be, and it still has placed commands over all human life. We see many who have an accurate knowledgeable recall of written biblical dialogue, but they appear themselves to be spiritually comatose, whereas they exemplify a stagnated spiritual connection to the Father through Jesus Christ?

Through our struggles to dominate and to control one another, it is obvious that we as human beings have agreed with one of the Lord's commandments to us as mankind; "to have dominion and to be in control in the earth." It is truly a reality that many people have believed that man was made to be the ruler in the earth, by way of their drives to take on wild untamable animals for pets, only to lose their lives as a result of the wild nature of the animals.

Even being explorers of the wild, having expeditions in all types of terrains, seas and the oceans it is soon realized that the wild has its place among men and the civilized humanity of man has been strategically set just outside of that of the jungle and the forest whereas, we were driven away from that style of living back in the garden, when as a result of the entrance of sin mankind and animals alike would take on an altered nature in the earth; we could no longer reside in the same habitats for living.

The assignment to conquer and to subdue, given to mankind by God from the beginning of creation was never intended to be only earthy and natural without the aid of the spirit of the Lord. So many people have fallen through the cracks of self exaltation seeing themselves as a lesser or an equal god or something bigger than life in the earth, seeking to take the control of other people and beast as well. Mere men don't seek only to be men of great godliness for the greater good of mankind; they are driven to be great even at the expense of their own lives!

Only without the spirit of the Lord working on the inside of us, do we fail to know the installed boundaries to our earthly limitations, even though some are more resilient than others; they can dive and even dig deeper, they can travel farther, faster; their process of thought is more fluid while their ability to accept explorative rewards of any search for truth are most gratifying.

People are looking and searching all of the time, and have even recorded the very same findings for their searches, as did others. Some, however, have chosen to look again disapproving of the initial findings, seeking an alternative reality to the previous find of their search. Even though people have searched the globe of the earth on the ground and in the sea, and the celestial, and the terrestrial dominance of space up in the sky having found nothing else that can replace the written word for truth, they still prefer to rest upon unfounded intellectual theories.

It is often the purpose of the pen to report what has been founded, whether true or false, to define and or document the truthful affirmation as a result of having looked inside of the written word for the researchers unfounded declarations of science personified. The pen looks into the word while the sword is the word of God; the sword is inside of the word already. The words of the pen talk about the written word, whereas the sword of the spirit is the written word, itself; speaking!

Any pen of its self cannot write alone without

the aid of a hand and the strength of an arm to manipulate the pen. Common since tells us that multiples upon multiples of words can be written with a single pen in the hand of a writer, but actually there are no installation of words in a single pen. The possibilities are endless as it relates to the innumerable types of words, languages, dialects, spellings, definitions, word levels and definitive comprehensive placements of words as it relates to the usage of the pen.

Write if you must, just know that your pen is powerless to reassign the purpose and the power of the word of God here in the earth. The assignment of the word of God has not even been totally fulfilled, even though it has been at least 92-96% fulfilled in the earth. The testament of the New Covenant in the word of God speaks to us today and is yet moving forward towards manifesting the total fulfillment of the scriptures.

The words of the scriptures are speaking out loud to all that will hear it, yet the arrogance of many won't allow themselves to hear the word of the Lord. Often the scripture states; "he that hath an ear to hear let him hear what the scripture saith unto the church!" The scripture speaks as if there are others hindering the possibilities for others to hear the word of our Lord.

Well, it just may be the power of your pen and the messages that you have composed that has run an interference with other individual's ability to hear the clarified message in the written word of God. What did you say? What did you tell your pen to write? What was it in your message that might have caused others to doubt the word of God; or maybe even to doubt the truthful reality of God altogether?

Wait!...................... To anyone that may write contrary in opposition to the written word of God; before patting yourselves on the back feeling a bit too successful in your ability to write, take into consideration the consequences for being so prolifically deterring in your own derogatory writing skills. Your swift ability of the pen may cause many to be swayed from their belief in God through the written word of God, but, however, the consequences for turning their minds will definitely be upon you.

You're accountable for all of the souls that are going to be lost as a result of your eager egotistical zeal to lend your opinionated authority to diffuse the saving power of the scriptures, knowing that you maintain a very hefty disbelief, disregard, and disdain for the scriptures.

Even the assignment of those who choose to disregard scripture and the authority of the written word of God should not be misdiagnosed or even misinterpreted. They have been allowed a voice of negative influence so as to provide real authentic selectiveness of choice and choosing. Without their penned opinions to the readers there would be no comparative dialogue to the truth; although they in my own opinion of the scripture are substance-less and empty having only logical/illogical explanations of their own failed research.

The originated assignment of the scripture is so assured that the Lord is not at all placed in a precarious position fearing the possibilities of faithful destructiveness among those who read as if the other written opinions have the power to eradicate the written accounts of the truth and the acts of God in the scripture.

> For ever, O Lord, thy word is settled in heaven. **Psalms 118: 80**

Mere men are satisfied with their ability to arouse questions in the minds of the readers of their materials. It is not wise to forget or even to give the benefit of the doubt to the truthful relevance over the fact that frustrated people miserably frustrate other people as well. Misery; still loves company; so since they choose not to believe the scripture knowing the penalty of their sinful unbelief, they strategically invite others to adjoin them in their declining persistence to fall away from the truth of the word of God.

Even though the accounts of the scripture have been penned and written into the biblical canonization of the scripture, it is however necessary to respect the fact that the accounts happened before they could ever have been written; with the exception to the prophetically spoken accounts that were to take place in future times. We have to admit that those things spoken prophetically did indeed come to pass with the undeniable accuracy to the written scriptures. As a matter of the fact there are some certain things of the scripture yet being fulfilled as of these late ages.

> So shall my word be that goeth forth out of my mouth: it shall not return unto me void, but it shall accomplish that which I please, and it shall

prosper in the thing whereto I send it. ***Isaiah 55: 11***

The word of God is set and totally affixed in chronic eternal obedience to the immutable will of God, therefore it cannot return unto the Lord void having never fulfilled its purpose leaving mankind's purpose in the earth disapproved, disappointed, and dissatisfied.

Knowing now that the word of God is obedient to the will of God without fail, having been assigned to be the defining establishment of our relationship with God, how is it that so many people are determined to disobey the word of God, yet claiming to be in harmonious fellowship with God?

The word of God is the most accurate thing that we have in this earth that will assure our eternal presence with God. Church people have the habit of doing a lot of stuff in the communities and in the churches alike, convincing themselves that God will have to take into account the things that they have done for other people while all of the time they had been rebellious to the written word of God.

Disobedience is not just some simple character flaw that many people have that God will overlook in the day of the judgment. The instructions for getting it right and getting things in line with God are only going to be found in the written word of God. I don't care what you do or the amount of money that you give to charities and churches, unless you obey the assigned word of God there is no way that you can make it to be with God in eternity.

*Understanding Assignments*

God is pleading with you right now to change! God won't be passing out excuses to those of you who just could not bring yourselves to obey the written word of God; (the bible), and neither will He be soft hearted and understanding because you have researched and had found that men wrote the bible. God knows who wrote the bible as it was their assignment from God to do so!

The biblical authors were assigned just as you and I are also assigned to do certain things in the earth for the sake of the kingdom of God, and for the purpose of humanity. It's your place and responsibility to find and to fulfill your purpose and to carry out your own assignment in the earth for the kingdom of God.

Church people effortlessly rebel to the commandments of God, but kingdom dwellers and seekers cannot even entertain the ideas of rebellion against the word of God.

Jesus taught us what we have come to know as the beattitudes (Matthew 5:); as people resist the even tide of change in the earth according to the written word of God, we the people of God have also been given the power of resistance against the resistance of the world to hold to our positions relative to the assignments that we have been given.

The beattitudes are the saints tune-up; they help us to get revved-up and to stay motivated in the face of opposition to our change and to the word of God!

Truly; Satan has no formidable answer to annihilate the assignments of man in the earth. Carrying out your ordained assignment can't be stopped! You have to give up and give in to the will of Satan, allowing him to dominate you for the purpose of his own devilish agenda; otherwise, he has no weapon against you that could ever prosper to defeat you and to overthrow your purpose in the earth as a believing obedient child and Son of God;

Complete your assignment............

# Chapter Two

# THE PURPOSE OF INTEGRITY

*Let me be weighed in an even balance, that God may know mine integrity.* **Job 31:6**
*The Lord shall judge the people: judge me, O Lord, according to thy righteousness, and according to mine integrity that is in me. Let integrity and uprightness preserve me; for I wait on thee. Judge me, O Lord; for I have walked in mine integrity: I have trusted also in the Lord; therefore I shall not slide. And as for me, thou upholdest me in mine integrity, and settest me before thy face forever.*
**Psalms 7:8; 25:21; 26:1; 41:12**

*Captured; Comprehensive; & Defined*

> *The integrity of the upright shall guide them: but the perverseness of the transgressors shall destroy them. The just man walketh in his integrity: his children are blessed after him.*
> **Proverbs 11:3, 20:7**

> *1. Possession of firm principles- the quality of possessing and steadfastly adhering to high moral principles or professional standards*
> *2. Completeness- the state of being complete or undivided*
> *3. Wholeness- the state of being sound or undamaged*

## Honesty, Truth, Truthfulness, Honor, Veracity, Reliability, Uprightness

### You Have It, Observe It*

The internal characteristical gauge; of by which an individual is rendered holistic and complete in humility and humanity; is integrity. Holistic people are trustworthy and forthright in all manner of their spirit and character. Those who observe integrity consistently in their behavior, are often more desirable to acquire the mirror image of God even in difficult times under the most intense pressure of extreme situations.

In general, most people are suggestively influenced through many other outside influences that we as a people alone of our own strength are incapable of standing against the onslaught of the

*The Purpose of Integrity*

most explicit detailed circumstances which come our way on a daily basis. Integrity announces our inner determination to withstand the power of attacking forces hurled against us, however; many are too weak having no displayed observance of integrity.

Exactly, what need is there for integrity if we are going to be forever too weak to handle the things in our lives? God has given us the power force of integrity in effect that we are able to choose the even greater power of the Holy Ghost should we discover that we are too indigent to put up a fight against the onslaught of the enemy. Integrity insures that we never find ourselves perpetrating and pretending that we are able to stand while all along we are sinking low and being defeated.

In all honesty and surety of faith and trust in God, integrity is there for us to ring the bell internally waking up the inner strength on the inside of our beings to fight for the respectfulness and character of our disposition before the people of our surroundings. Integrity insures that we respect ourselves so that we will never allow ourselves to be publically embarrassed or even outwardly disgraced. Integrity even takes on an even more heightened position within us once we have been saved and filled with the spirit of the Lord, whereas we never show up totally weakened ever again.

*I can [I will]; do all things through Christ which strenghtenth me.*
*Emphasis added* **Philippians 4:13**

Do you have it? Do you even know what it is? How do you know that you actually observe integrity; and what makes you so sure that others around you are not observing integrity unless you are sure that you know what it is?  Integrity is a personal characteristical trait of quality inborn into the nature of every person from birth, whereas a parent only has to nudge the child to get them to recognize the trait and to get them to use it thus building a foundation for excellence.

Integrity is not to be respected as being the identifiable trait of any social group in society; it is not even to be ascertained with being an award of any church respectively; having finances, good credit, better paying jobs, or living in a neighborhood that has the most expensive homes; these things are only the resulting benefits of integrity.  Should any of these things be lost, integrity would follow the departure of those things and be gone or lost as a result.

Only because we as a society of people have lost respect for the observance of integrity, is the reason that people can't really say that they even know what true integrity is.  We know that things are not what they used to be and we realize that the changes took place right under our noses so fast that we really didn't recognize the dissimilarity until we were in the vortex of the popular distortion.  The control slipped right out from beneath our immediate grasp as the requirement for integrity lessened.

The issue of integrity or the lack thereof, seems to arise more so in these latter times especially in the churches.  The truth is that many of the churches are operating on zero base levels of integrity, the business dealings are to the likes of the characteristics of the "Adams Family" they do what want to do, say what they want to say, despising accountability at all points of references having no since of caring for what is thought about them or even reported on them in public forums and in the media.

Of course we hear of things taking place in and around the local churches that we never even dreamed would ever be happening in the churches, for sure. Starting from the top of the religious spectrum of the churches, many of the leaders are leaving off from being respectable leaders with much integrity to being declared as an "Iconic" figure among the people of even the secular society. So many of the preachers are play preaching in the pulpits, making it easy for them to play preach on the movie screens nowadays.

Though despised of most people of the secular society, almost always you could tell the difference in direct contrast to the leaders of the churches and the secular leaders of the society because of the conviction and the strong unchangeable character of integrity. You knew that both sets of the leaders were seeking to influence the people in accordance to the adherence of their chosen agendas or mandates for daily living, both personally and in the community. Now it is not easily detected whether the minister is a preacher of the gospel of Jesus Christ or a politician running for public office.

There were some certain things that a public leader would not say over a public address system for the simple reason of respect and the observance of integrity within themselves and respectively to the intent of not offending the integrity of others.

The nightly news broadcast, and even the evening news broadcast were also very careful of the content that they reported and definitely of the images that they allowed to be seen during their broadcast.

For an instance: in light of a homicide; the most that you would see over the television or even pictured in the local news paper was a body of the deceased covered with a white sheet either laying on the ground or atop of a gurney still covered from head to toe, and if they could help it you almost never saw blood! Now you might see blood and guts, bulging eyeballs, lacerated throats, and even dismembered bodies if they are able to get it in. Certain media broadcast stations will even put up with being fined just to be able to show the blood and gore to the television viewers.

Radio Disc-jockeys were also equally as careful not to allow certain disrespectful content to be aired over the radio all on the strength of integrity without hesitation whereas most of the people of the media did do so without murmuring and complaining, it was just the kind of things that you did because you had respect for and the observance of integrity. Of course now the recording industry and record producers have forced the hands of the radio stations and they have no choice but to play the racy raunchy content of R & B, and Hip Hop artist alike.

The overt spiritual flavor of gospel music, which was harder labeled as "church music" made listening more easily recognizable for the believer and the clubhouse dancers to differentiate in respect to their own chosen genres. Gospel music kept you in mind of the church at all times as result of hearing it over the radio, now there is barely no difference heard in the music as those who are purportedly gospel music artist have given up on the integrity of the spirit of Christ for a much higher paycheck for their music.

Gospel music artist seem to feel that certain since of arrival when they have had their music played in the popular night clubs and on secular radio stations across the country and even across the globe even whenever their music is not at all being played in the churches or during religious broadcasting. Songwriters have even begun to omit the mention of the name of Jesus in their music so as to create a cross-over tune whereas the song can be taken an enjoyed by any listener no matter of their system of belief or their purported behavioral patterns.

We use to have authentic mobile service stations where you bought gas, had tires repaired, bought new tires, got the oil checked and changed, they checked all of the fluid levels of the automobile and even washed the windows as a courtesy in appreciation for your patronage of their service station all on the strength of integrity, now we have convenience stores with self service gas pumps where you serve yourself or do without; being that people lost respect for public servants.

I can remember when the milk man delivered the milk to the house and placed it out on the front porch at a certain time every week whereas it wasn't common for anyone to bother that which had been personally delivered to your home. The dairy delivery was also compensated at a certain time of the month; they had trust and respect for the integrity of their patrons. Now we have dairy stores specifically that also carry produce which is even long since before now, an upgrade from the dairy and the produce sections in the grocery stores.

Doctors used to make home visits to administer medicine and to treat medical emergencies, and sometimes they may have even performed minor surgeries. Physicians use to carry medical bags with syringes and other operational tools and certain medicines for the average individual who may not have had certain allergies to medicine and could be carefully administered at home. The doctor's house calls were carried out on the strength of the integrity of the patients and the physicians alike; people use to believe in integrity!

## I Know What Integrity is...

We all started out with this one enormous quality as individuals even though many of us did not even know that it existed, unless we had parents that were people who observed the moral fortitude of integrity. It's simple, as we have been taught the biblical principle of the golden rule which states; "do unto others, as you would have them do unto you," following this simple little rule establishes a foundational platform underneath the actuality of the observance of integrity.

I have always understood integrity to be that quality within an individual that seeks to preserve, to maintain, and even to work as a bonding seal of protection between two people, business deals, social or business proposals, or simply to act as the watchman between us while we were absent one from another. Integrity to me is that working order

*The Purpose of Integrity*

on the inside of us down in our bellies that illiminates the need for having someone watch over us standing over our backs to ensure that we operate honestly. Integrity makes sure that I don't cheat others when my word of promise has been given.

Coming up as a young boy, whenever we didn't trust one of our friends, or we didn't believe a story that we were being told, we would say to them "do you swear on a stack of bibles?" If or when they replied to us that they would do so, most of the time that was enough. Other times we would actually go and get a bible or two for them to place their hands upon like as in the presence of a Judge in a courtroom being sworn in to give a testimony.

Sometimes we had other little sayings to take up an oath of honesty, promising that we were telling the truth. We would say; "Hope to die; Stick a Needle in my eye!" "I swear on my grandmother's grave!" In other words, we wanted you to know that we were telling you the whole truth and nothing but the truth! Mind you that we were children in the neighborhood handling things our own way. At those times, we were definitely ignorant to the real meaning in the word of God concerning swearing and taking an oath.

It was more of a neighborhood pledge of truth to one another! We watched little shows like the "Little Rascals" and other cartoons whereas friends stuck together at all cost; so they made vows and pledged their trust to one another. The things that are most memorable to me are the terrible feelings of having been lied to or deceived by someone from the group that had pledged to be truthful to everyone, and the loss of trust and the desire of the group to sever the ties as friends. If they had only been honest everything would have been left intact.

I am of the opinion that the writers of the shows back then were in their own ways trying to teach us the principles of integrity although they did not call it that; it may have been for the sake of allowing our parents the privileges and the opportunities to teach us what integrity was and how it is to be applied to our lives daily. I have come to realize now although we were going about it all the wrong way, that we were trying to teach our neighborhood friends and loved ones to observe and to maintain integrity.

### The Good Suffer With The Bad

Now it's past time for us in the body of Christ to line up with the word of God and begin to behave our selves like we really do know the Lord in our own individual lives. It is not just that the bad people are in the midst of the good, (quote un quote), the problem is really that the people who are supposedly the good people of the church and the surrounding communities, are also the ones responsible for acting up as if they had never been changed.

I had a conversation with a very good friend of mine about prominent Pastors of the churches that use profanity on a consistent basis. One real hilarious report that I was given of one of the foul mouthed Christian confessing brothers was that, he talked slow so as to keep a watch on what he'd say, in that he might have the mental fortitude to catch the profanity before it slipped out of his mouth in the church, right from the platform of the pulpit.

### That's Crazy!

Of course I have been told of very true occurrences of which ministers used profanity ( 4 letter words) in the pulpit during a sermonic delivery; where's the integrity in that? The preachers all reported most of them anyway, that the profanity slipped out of their mouths in the pulpit, of which is indicative of saying to me that it would not have been a slippage had it not been in the church or in the pulpit!

Such occurrences does not bespeak of the fact that one had forgotten where they were or of whom it is that they are supposed to be in the Lord and to the church; but, it does suggest that there is absolutely no respectful observance of integrity, nor any respect of self thereof. It is very difficult to escape being who you are on a daily basis just because you have entered the church building. God sees us and He knows who we are 24/7, too often people forget that it is God that matters most in reference to our true character. We can't fool God!

As a result of the misguided behavior of those leading personnel of the churches, it has caused a massive suspicion to be cast over all of the leaders, and in many situations the general populous of the churches at large are now held suspect to the possible perpetration of fraudulent behavior, even though they are doing everything in their own strength and power to live the life that they sing and shout about.

Not everyone is a fake or a dangerous pretender; purporting to know Christ when in fact they have never been saved from the life of sin and shame. Many times those who have been changed by the shed blood of Christ, suffer the negative feedback and the backlashes of the disgruntled people of the communities and of the churches who had been deceived or otherwise hurt by other unreal people.

I often wonder why it is that they hardly seem to take their complaints to those people that had done them wrong? Rather, they make sure to wreak havoc on as many people of the churches in general as possible. The entire spectrum of the church has been convicted and sentenced to hell and to the, "*I told you so*" syndrome of the doubters and the hateful unbelievers of the society.

Were it not for the truth of God in Christ Jesus the church as we know of it today would no longer be standing. Only because there are real true believers in the churches, is it impossible for the secular media and society to totally annihilate the influence of the local church at large, thus rendering the world as a godless societal influence.

Wherever mere men are in control the good suffer with the bad for the sake of the fact that people are indigent of true justice and judgment. We've seen it over and over again, where the good suffer with bad! When the actual culprits cannot be held accountable for their wrong actions, whether of sins or crimes; or even sinful crimes; everyone has to suffer the penalty for the hidden perpetrators.

These are no new occurrences of this present generation alone, rather it has been going on for many centuries. Somehow man has a method of penalizing everybody in an effort to get to the right one, although they have often failed to effectively send the message to the guilty parties for

*The Purpose of Integrity*

their wrong doing. God is able to do what no other manner of authority could ever do!

We have walked around in shame at the fact the we have leaders who live out loud, dangerously damaging the image of the churches without a care or any since of remorse for their outlandish behavior. As it is we who are of the church have given our focal points to the wrong images of the churches even assigning that which is clearly ungodly and non-biblical as having been sent into the church by God.

We often suffer the harsh criticism of the community for the simple fact that so many of the people have learned the art of covering up for the wrong doing of those of the churches who should have been changed from living sinful, except for those who are not of a certain clique or group! I have not met many people who don't mind suffering anything as it is! The mindset of most people is to avoid everything that might cause any unrest or adverse situations that set us back or even shut us out of whatever we may deem as forward progress, especially in the churches.

For this reason along I'm appalled at the attitudes of the people who are so determined to reject the deity of Christ, seeing that He suffered on the cross of Calvary. One thing for sure which might have gotten lost in translation is the fact that Jesus suffered the things that we should have, so that we would not have to. The things that we suffer are of no comparison to what Christ suffered during the crucifixion.

*49*

*Captured; Comprehensive; & Defined*

### Integrity to the Finish*

In the final analysis of integrity, it is clear to me now that we are given the powerful input of integrity to ensure that we are able to finish that which has been assigned to us in this life of which we are living. I have always believed that God believes in humanity, and that He's sure that we can do whatever He has assigned our hands to do. I was just a bit foggy in my understanding as to how the surety was indeed levied within the makeup of the humanistic purposeful cause.

The people of today look to the people of yesterday's bible historical accountants to assign a more integral aspect to their relationship with God the Father; believing that they must have been built stronger and more powerful than that of those of us who live today. Many believe that Abraham, Isaac, and Jacob, the three Hebrew boys and Daniel, Samson, Samuel, David and Job; that perhaps they had something more unique in their DNA profile that allowed them to be seriously dedicated to the Lord thus rendering them supernaturally more powerful than we of today?

Perhaps they only had fewer choices for denying the integrity on the inside of them than we have today? It might have even been that they had already climbed the foolish hills of life living outside of the will of God by the time that we had heard of them in the scriptural accounts? Whatever the case, the fact is that they all observed integrity of their spirit and character before the Lord.

Remember, the wife of Job thought that he was definitely overboard in his own integrity before the Lord during the time of his trials; she wanted

Job to accept in his heart that God had forsaken him, and therefore do as other barbaric men had done, and curse God and die! Her question to her husband was; "Do you still maintain your integrity towards God?"

However, it was indeed because of the integrity of Job that he made it successfully to the end of his trials, and received double for all of his troubles! Integrity allowed Job to finish with his head held high; though he had been embarrassed and falsely accused by his own friends of being a sinner who had angered God; Satan himself, accused Job of not being strong enough to handle what was about to come upon him.

But, my friends, it was God Himself that testified of the integrity of Job; God told Satan that Job was the most upright man in the land of Uz. In paraphrasing; God told Satan to take his best shots against Job, and that he would prove to him that Job could not be turned from following after the will and the ways of God. In the final analysis God is always right, even when it relates to us of today; God always knows about our integrity.

It is through the strength and the power of integrity that we are able to flow about and within the business of the kingdom of God and to get it finished before we' as individuals singly press our heads against a dying pillow to fall asleep in death. Integrity has the power to eradicate all of the possibilities of hypocrisy and fraudulent behavior in and throughout the kingdom of God worldwide.

I love the fact that we do not have to either put on or step into integrity, it is simply ingrained within our individual makeup and character sketch.

*Captured; Comprehensive; & Defined*

From the very moment that we are aware of the differences between right; and wrong; and are able to make the decision of proper choices, the vibrant power of integrity is activated within us, moving us to respectfully focus on our character.

Integrity consistently shines the spotlight within me, whereas I am constantly aware of the actual condition of myself from within me. Yes, that's right, all of us know who we are from the inside out and from the outside in; but it's our choice whether or not we are going to pay attention to the discovery of the finds within ourselves.

Integrity forces me to focus on the missing parts and the broken places within me so as not to allow family members and friends to discourage me by encouraging me to turn away from my place in God. Alike Job's wife; those who are closest to us are the ones who will be most apt to try and attempt to show us that we are perhaps too serious about living for God! Certain people will always want to suggest that you live a little and lower the Christian standard in your own living atmosphere so that others are more comfortable around you.

As a young boy in the Baptist church, we used to sing a song that said; "we are soldiers, in the army, we have to fight, although we have to cry, we have to hold up the blood stained banner, we have to hold it up until we die!"

Integrity forces me to stay in the fight and to never give up, even though the odds are against me. When my so-called friends are pointing their fingers at me, and saying that I will never be able to succeed, it's the integrity on the inside of me which drives me to continue on to the finish.

*The Purpose of Integrity*

Integrity makes since of the fact that I believe in myself! Integrity ensures me that even when others have ceased to believe in me, that it really is okay to continue to believe, and to keep moving up the king's highway. Integrity is the assurance of my faith in God, because it causes me to check myself to be sure that I really do believe according to the written word of God.

Integrity at its greatest works like so: whatever I say to you that I am going to do, according to my true ability to get it done, I will do everything in my own power to make sure that it happens. Jesus said to the Father; prepare for me a body, and I will go down and redeem man, and He came to the earth, born of a virgin, grew in stature and in the favor of God, He went to the Cross of Calvary, shed His own blood, He died and was buried in a borrowed tomb, and was raised on the third day, God raised Him up!

If Jesus had no integrity God would never have raised Him from the grave. Jesus did just what He said; God said just what Jesus did; as a result we are here today to reap the victory! On the cross Jesus said; it is finished! Upon doing so, the finishing touches were added to mankind so that the human assignment at large could be accomplished without fail in the entire earth………………………………

Now that you understand integrity; show what's on the inside of you to those who are surrounding you. Either you've got it or you don't! What about you? Do you really have it? Check Yourself; you might have been lacking Integrity all along!

# Chapter Three
# ON THE PREMISE OF THE BLOOD

*And the Lord God formed man from the dust of the ground, and breathed into his nostrils the breath of life: and man became a living soul*
.                    **Genesis 2: 7**
*And the Lord said unto Cain, where is Abel thy brother? And he said, I know not: Am I my brother's keeper? And He said, what hast thou done? The voice of thy brother's blood crieth unto me from the ground. And now art thou cursed from the earth, which hath open her mouth to receive thy brother's blood from thy hand;*
                    **Genesis 4: 9-11**

*Captured; Comprehensive; & Defined*

For the life of the flesh is in the blood: and I have given it to you upon the alter to make an atonement for your souls: for it is the blood that maketh an atonement for the soul. For it is the life of all flesh; the blood of it is for the life thereof: therefore I said unto the children of Israel, Ye shall not eat the blood of no manner of flesh: for the life of all flesh is the blood thereof: whosoever eateth it shall be cut off. **Leviticus 17: 11, 14** And when I passed by thee, and saw thee polluted in thine own blood. I said unto thee when thou wast in thy own blood, Live; yea, I said unto thee when thou wast in thy own blood, Live.
**Ezekiel 16:6**

PREMISES - LAW MATTERS PREVIOUSLY STATED OR REFERRED TO IN A LEGAL DOCUMENT SUCH AS A DEED PREMISE - BASIS OF AN ARGUMENT - A PROPOSITION THAT FORMS THE BASIS OF AN ARGUMENT OR FROM WHICH A CONCLUSION IS DRAWN; [I QUESTION THE PREMISE ON WHICH YOUR WHOLE THEORY IS BASED.] SOMETHING ON THE FOUNDATION OF A PROPOSITION OR IDEA; STATED OR ASSUMED TO BE TRUE; TRANSITIVE VERB TO STATE SOMETHING IN ADVANCE TO INTRODUCE OR EXPLAIN WHAT FOLLOWS

## On Blood Establishment

It is universally recognized and realized that the living are alive through the agility and mobile uprighted activity of the physical body, as we bend our joints and reproduce offspring after our own kind; all on the involuntary impulse to inhale and to expel taken breaths of air. It's been the common practicality of people, even of today, to disregard the blood infusion of the veins and arteries of our bodies which was indeed God's method of giving life to humanity, as the life of all flesh is in the blood! No one will ever live without blood in their body.

Our present understanding of the most recent contact with dust was that the dust is dry and incapable of being manipulated to form anything, especially human? As human beings, we are grossly baffled at the idea of being formed from the dust of the ground, however, we are able to relate to the dryness of all-purpose flower in that how it is also very dry and incapable of sticking together adhesively to form bread, cakes and other food substances standing along absent of the other added ingredients.

It has been scientifically proven that the human body is 87% consistency of water, of which is acceptable in science laboratories all across the globe. If the body were consistent of only just dust, I'm sure that I could fathom the argument of modern science and other skeptics of biblical accounts and of faith in God. But it behooves us to come to the understanding that something other than just dust was added by God to make up the human consistency.

The dust of the ground being combined with the water of the earth was formed and manipulated by the spirit, through the will of God to make skin, flesh and hair. The contentious struggle is found within the fact that the human body is 100% a God creation, whereas the only method of duplicating the make-up of mankind is through the God ordained process of procreation of the enjoined communal copulation of the man and the woman.

God; has purposed within the total makeup of Human consistency in mankind, that we accept and embrace who we are, not that we should spend our existence on the face of the earth trying to figure out how God manipulated the dust from the ground to make us. How God formed me is His business, it's my business to just simply be who I am.

> And there are three that bear witness in the earth, the spirit, and the water, and the blood: and these three agree in one. **I John 5: 8**

Further receiving the breath of life from our maker and creator, after being created and formed from the dust from the ground, questions have arrived and have been frequently asked, such as; "where did our blood come from?" You should understand that at the very same instance, God infused the body simultaneously as He gave it breath. The blood was there in the beginning with God.

Just as sap was already in the trees as they grew up out of the earth, and the chlorophyll was already in its green leaves to provide the purification of the exhaled carbon dioxide to transform it into fresh breaths of air to breathe; you will never witness a baby born alive without blood in its veins as there would be no life to cause the body to live. Doesn't matter who the father is or isn't, somebody's blood will have to be running through the veins and the arteries in the body of that child.

While many Theologians have argued over the missing human facts of whom Jesus' natural father could have been; the over-looked fact is that there was definitely blood in His veins at birth. The most important fact of the crucifixion of the cross of Calvary was indeed the shedding of the Blood of Jesus! No doubt about it, Jesus, definitely had blood in His veins.

Modern science may in fact be intelligent, but they will not discover ways for the body to live without blood. It is the life in the blood which tells the body to breathe and to take in a breath of air, and to expel the used air back out into the atmosphere. If Scientist were successful to invent a true blood substitute, they would find that they are incapable of producing a compatible life substitute, of which is the spirit of life in the blood that allows the body to live upright in an erect posture upon its feet with its head towards the sky having the natural God given activities of the body in normal functionality.

The air that we breathe into our lungs does not even reach our brains without the proper blood flow in the body from the head to toe. Contaminated and even distorted blood may often mean the end of life in the body, whereas the health of the blood is in extreme jeopardy, indigent to sustain and to maintain living in the body! We need good blood running through our veins that is conducive for the proper function of the vital organs on the inside of us. The vital organs of the body cannot live and function normally being poisoned and contaminated by sick blood passing through them.

Blood disorders have taken place only since the fall of man, at the entrance of sin and iniquity. As we explore the premise of the blood; we come to rest upon the point of realizing that it was all a blood thing with God even before the beginning. Our minds have been blown out of proportion as we attempt to comprehend the reason that God is so seriously unwavering when it comes to the issue of the blood.

I'm talking about the actual establishment of mankind, not the establishment of the earth! We know what the word of God says about the foundational establishment of the land and the sea from the beginning of the existence of mankind in the earth. Very religiously we quote the scripture, "man cannot live by bread alone, but by every word that proceedeth out of the mouth of God;" but without the blood, mankind would not even be alive to eat bread!

We as living creatures upon the face of the earth are consistently moving and breathing without being connected to any electrical cords extending to power outlets like lamps and other electronic mechanisms. The blood naturally rejuvenates itself through proper diet and sufficient rest. The blood doesn't have to be medicated and scientifically programmed to be rejuvenated or even replenished; not normally anyway.

God so awesomely conditioned the body to cleanse the blood through the liver and kidneys, and to nourish the health of the body through the aid of the pancreas, digestive system and intestines, but all through the passing of the blood flow in and throughout the body. We have smart blood flowing through our bodies!

What other entity could there have ever been out there in space or even in the ocean, to infuse the natural intelligence into the blood plasma to tell the blood which way to flow in the body and where to pick up the oxygen in the body to carry it to the brain and to aid the body in living? The very power of the blood is Life; but the very purpose of the blood is to generate living in the body.

## The Exact House of Life

The real me who looks out of my eyes and into a mirror to see my own natural figure, is living on the inside of me alive in my own blood-stream. Although you may be allowed to observe me for years and months on end, there are elements of the true character of my spirit inside of me that you are never going to be able to see with natural eyesight.

The actual house of truth and reality for which we live our daily lives is located in the blood which flows through the veins in our bodies. I have discovered through biblical revelations, and of course from medical science observations that we are no more alive than the actual flow of the blood in our veins. When the circulation of the blood in our bodies ceases to flow, all vital signs of living also cease and stop.

Should the veins be lacerated or otherwise opened on purpose or by accident, whereas the blood is allowed to flow outward draining from the body, the identifiable personality of the human body is also released leaving the soul homeless. We are allotted only mere minutes, dependent upon which vein or artery has been lacerated, before the body will literally bleed to death and begin the process of decaying and rotting its way back to the dust of the earth from which it came.

It is time that we come to the point of understanding the exact purpose for living in our natural bodies. Our bodies are constructed to achieve the true purpose for which our blood has been charged to activate living. Our bodies aid in giving recognition to the living reality of our individual identities while we exist on the face of the earth. It is paramount that we; as an individual, be recognized for the exact person that we are.

The true mystical human identity is found within the blood of every individual person. My blood tells me who I am, my gender, the genealogy of my family, the health history, and much more............ Only, the true spirit and character of who we really are is housed in the flow of the bloodstream in our veins.

God knows who we are without mistake based on the blood in our veins, as people are now prone to have facial alterations, and sexual gender change operations, and other surgical manipulations which alter the actual image to modify the visible physique of their individual personhood. However, our blood must remain the very same as it were from the times of our natural birth. Doesn't matter if we have come to despise our parents, who we are relative to the blood in our bodies, will forever yield the identifiable traits of our true family identity?

Life also seizes the grip of death not allowing it to take hold of an individual until God says so. Death itself can have no claim to a body whose blood is continuously filled and fused with the spirit of life. For as long as there is life in the blood, the body must refuse to die. We that are alive and postured upright in position on our feet, our activities are internalizes in the life in the blood.

You may question then how is it possible that so many people have dead inactive limbs attached their bodies, yet they are still alive? Often the limbs are in a paralyzed state, whereas it cannot actually die and be totally dead for as long as the blood continues to flow to those limbs. Many people who have paralyzed limbs often complain of intense pains in those same limbs; death has no feelings at all. But as soon as there is no blood flow to any particular limb, the limb dies and gangrene will set in, in which the dead limb is attached to an alive body! The only viable answer is that the blood has ceased to flow to those limbs, giving way to the livid inactivity;

If ever the blood flow could again be increased to those dying portions of the body, those limbs would again regain live activity, usefully responding to the operational command of the individual's body. Whenever God commands the blood to again flow to those once denied areas of the body, through faith in the infallable word of God; miraculously it causes those areas to live again.

Life in and of itself is endless, like unto the endless reign of eternity and God who is the giver and the creator of life. We will continue life eternally in the spirit realm in Heaven with the Father, or in Hell; this is a truthful reality. Life; exits the blood at the existing end of the living; whereas the blood can still be in the body, but it will have ceased to flow through the body as it did during the natural functionality of the living body. Death is not the total eradication of life; while it does end living naturally in the body; as life cannot die.

The bloodstream becomes an empty home, incapable of sustaining a living body; those who answered the call of their given names have now expired their allotted time of living on earth and have transitioned, no longer available to respond to being called upon. All that is left behind of the given natural forms are the empty shells and past memories of the once alive individuals who lived in them.

The dreadful reality for many people has been the diagnosis of poorly maintained blood-health; Most do not even consider or even intentionally care for the very necessary health of the blood until they have been informed that their blood is actually in the poorest of condition. In other words, they intentionally avoid eating foods and consuming beverages that possibly ensure the health of the blood.

See; I get it now! Bad and fatty food choices have an effect in the blood which causes it to become cluttered and clogged thus rendering the blood to become poorly oxygenated, whereas the blood is no longer at its originated function to generate vigorous energetic living as originally designed. Often under such poor dietary maintenance of the body and the blood, the bloodstream becomes high-jacked; overtaken by adverse possibilities of annihilation and destruction.

The blood is smart in that it has the ability to deposit the nutrients to the proper places in the body, but, when the vital organs of the body are already filled to the optimum levels, the foreign particles in the blood become unwanted passengers, riding in the flow of the blood stream having nowhere in the body to get off the ride. High-Jacked in broad daylight! Blood-Jacked while dining!

Blood itself must breathe carrying oxygen to the vital organs of the body so that the body can live. Blood starved of its needed supply of oxygen, will break-down separating the normal blood particles and cells, fragmenting the red blood cells from the white blood cells, demolishing the given bloodhouse of life in any individual due to the alien objects attaching itself to the blood-cell walls.

I personally believe that it was God's original

intention that we'd be eternally sustained with the life of the blood on the inside of us which was possibly of an eternal quality in its originated state, but because of sin and iniquity the blood of humanity was forever contaminated and no longer sufficient to eternally sustain the life given to humanity.

Therefore, we have the alternate benefit and the eternal blessing of being submerged beneath the blood of Jesus Christ that can never lose its power to both give and to sustain life eternally!

### Curiosity; Spilled the Blood**

The first recorded incident of an intentional blood spill was documented in Genesis chapter 4; whereas Cain rose up against his own brother Abel in the field and killed him. We know that the death of Abel was Satan's idea of which he had implanted in to the heart and the mind of Cain, because when questioned by God; Cain lied immediately! The originated spirit of Cain would have truthfully said; he is there in the ground, I buried him there! He was aware that God already knew what he had done to and with his own brother.

It is obvious that mankind gleaned the ability to kill from this murderous incident and the location for doing it, as it is often reported that someone has been murder in the field or either they had been dumped in the field after being murdered.

What is precariously misread in the biblical dialogue of the tragedy of these two brothers of the first family of the earth was the blood spill! You ever wonder why Cain didn't just suffocate his brother until he could no longer breathe? Had it been done so that he had only denied his brother's air supply, Satan's curiosity to examine the bloods capacity to activate human living would not have been so realistically denied as it had already been so affixed by God.

The murder of Abel was Satan's idea, according to St. John 8:44, the liar and the deceiver. Jesus said that Satan was a murderer from the beginning! Satan talked with Cain and Cain talked with Abel and carried out Satan's plot against him. Satan had an interest in the blood that only permanently infuriated him from now on, simply for the fact that he would never have any life giving authority or the denial of living; manipulating the blood!

Whatever Satan does, he is often trying to duplicate or to imitate what God has already done although he is unsuccessful! God; in His infinite wisdom, had already shut up the ground the very moment that it became apparent that Adam and Eve had indeed sinned in the garden. God shut out Satan's ability to go back into the ground to create his own prototype and species, using God's methods to do so.

Satan was able to see God at work as he skillfully fashioned and formed man from the dust of the earth, from the ground later infusing the arteries and the veins of man with the breath of life, of which was the blood and the air. Satan was familiar with the air, but he had never seen the blood before God breathed it into living beings in the earth.

The inquisitiveness of Satan drove him to launch after the creative composition in the blood of his own replacements of worship and praise of our God; knowing that there were no other created beings in the earth like God other than man.

Don't be fooled, Satan knew that mankind had something in them that even the Angels of the Lord, and of those fallen angels which fell with him, and that he himself did not even have, which was blood! What's more, was the fact that Satan knew that the blood on the inside of mankind was pleasing in the sight of God.

If there were ever going to be a possibility of really extinguishing mankind, some way or another he was going to have to figure out how to separate life from the blood, of which was later on the Satanic discovery of death of the human body form. Satan saw that the man formed did not even stand erect on his feet and begin to move about the earth until the blood activated life and caused him to live.

Satan was unaware that the murderous action taken against Cain was death until God told him, and neither did he even know that the blood was spilled out until the blood began to speak out to the Father from the ground! I believe that Satan thought that he could do what God had done with the blood in the dust of the ground, which was to bring forth living beings. Perhaps Satan even believed that Abel would leap upwards and live again, once his own blood had hit the ground? After all he had seen the Father activate living through the infusion of the blood in the formed man from the dust of the ground.

But God! The blood would never again be placed in the ground to cause living beings to come forth ever again. As a result, the blood of a humanity found itself in a place now forbidden among humanity.

Satan is still curiously grappling with the life of the blood and its ability to cause mankind to feel and to know, moving about in all the earth with dominating authority and the ability to communicate with God in heaven, having been created lower beings than the angels. The awe striking abilities and amenities of the life of humanity are incomparable to anything else that had ever been done in all the created realm of the earth and the spiritual realm.

Every action of Satan since the fall from heaven has always been infused with the insane ability to displease God. His first displeasing act in the earth against mankind was at the tree in the midst of the garden, where he caused man to sever the spiritual relationship with God for a time being, whereas mankind would spend the rest of their natural lives seeking atonement for the broken fellowship with God.

Many have been declared unclean and highly infectious to contaminate the cleaner portions of the population unless they are quarantined in isolation away from the general populous. No one wants to even be in the vicinity of a person that is bleeding out openly as those who are bleeding are often regarded as being dangerous to others.

Certain blood contaminations will change the total scope of living for many who had even been thought of as the more well being individuals of society. One could be very wealthy and rich in financial gain and accummulated assets but have a serious contamination in their blood and most people wouldn't even want to touch their money! Blood illness is to be taken as a sure threat to living and being able to remain alive. Contaminated blood is a sure cause for shortened life spans in these latter times.

## Coagulated Blood***

Ever since the creation and the formidable design of mankind from the dust of the ground, God intentionally set the scale to the balance of the blood for living according to every individual Species of Birds and Beast, Kinds of Fishes and Mammals, and finally also for the livelihood of the diverse Hues of all Mankind over the entire face of the earth.

Perhaps the illustrative revelations are coming into focus now to allow for even greater understanding as to why it is that God has been so serious about the blood, and especially the blood of Jesus! As a result of the blood the status for our spiritual welfare and realignment for the atonement is exclusively the purpose for the blood of Jesus before His blood was shed on Calvary and even before He ever left Heaven to come to the earth.

Back when the children of Israel were being delivered from their captivity to the Egyptians, the final plague was that God would touch the first born of all living beings in Egypt because of the hardness of the heart of Pharaoh. God said to Moses; sprinkle the blood over the lintel of every doorpost of the children of Israel, and when I see the blood I will pass over that household and not allow death to touch the first born of that household.

Wherever life was signified through the displaying of blood on the doorpost it was the ultimate indication that the people chose to live adhering to their faith in God. God's sight was, and it has always been set on life and not just the living; He would be killing the firstborn of those that were associated to the wickedness of the Egyptians which had also rejected God through the lifestyle of their own signs and wonder seeking curiosity rejecting the signs and wonders which God wrought through Moses and his anointed rod.

The Prophet Ezekiel picks up on the ministry in the message of the blood later on as the centuries had passed when the hand of the Lord was upon Him commanding him to prophesy of the status of the rebellious generations of Israel. God began to show the Prophet Ezekiel the former conditions of Israel and how it was that He had delivered them through the power of the blood from bondage and captivity to Pharaoh and the Egyptians.

God told Moses to touch the river of Egypt with the tip of the rod in his hand and all of the waters in Egypt immediately turned to blood? The fish in the waters all died belly up in the blood stained rivers of water, the cattle in the fields died as result of having no water to drink, and such was the plight of all of the animal life in Egypt.

Even the water in the water pitchers poured out as blood whereas there was no water for drinking in all of Egypt! Perhaps it was God's own method of blood-washing sinful, evil, and God rejecting Egypt for which God Himself would not have to totally erase Egypt from the face of the earth as in the case of Sodom and Gamorrah and the surrounding cities!

The massive show of blood as one of the deadlier plagues in Egypt was definitely a reminder to Pharaoh and to all of the Egyptians of the four hundred years of bloodshed of the Israelites while in captivity. Enough blood had been shed to consume and to kill off all of the life forms in Egypt, God was saying to Egypt; that He had not forgotten what they had done cruelly to the captive Israelites shedding their innocent blood.

God revealed to both Egypt and to Israel the power of the blood even before He told Moses to place the blood over the lintel of the doorpost. It's always been a blood thing with God!

However, this word of prophecy to the Prophet Ezekiel was not just an admonishment to that group of present day Israelites of his own contemporaries; but is was also a prophetic foretelling of the total deliverance of the people of the earth. God let us know that He would have to bathe the people of the earth in the pure blood of Jesus Christ, thus restoring the fellowship and the relationship of mankind and God.

> And when I passed by thee, and saw thee polluted in thine own blood. I said unto thee when thou wast in thy own blood, Live; yea, I said unto thee when thou wast in thy own blood, Live.
> **Ezekiel 16:6**

Throughout the reign of humanity, mankind has gotten further and further polluted and contaminated in his own blood. Sin and iniquity still pollutes the blood both naturally and spiritually, to the point that many people do not even wish to have their own blood in their blood streams.

As many take on blood transfusions, the blood must be matched to the exact type of the blood flowing in the body already. Cross-matching blood types can prove fatal to the recipients, where the body is already receptive to its original blood-life type.

Therefore, Jesus bore and carried the blood of humanity at large as given from the Father of all created Human Beings; Mankind; allowing His blood to position us rather than to poison us. Just as the blood was fatal to the Egyptians during the plague, the wrong blood type is fatal to all human beings and to animals.

Had Jesus been the natural son of an earthly father who had been a Jew, or a Hebrew; his blood would not have been sufficient for the redemption

*Captured; Comprehensive; & Defined*

of humanity at large. No earthly father could do it simply because of the fact that all people of the earth had been sinfully infected and forever contaminated with the nature of sin from the garden.

The Levitical Priesthood was ordered of the Lord to provide a blood sacrifice for the atonement of all mankind to be offered upon the altar of sacrifice for the sins of humanity. The blood would be sprinkled from the doorway of the Tabernacle to the Mercy Seat on the Arc of the Covenant behind the veil of the temple in the Holies of Holy.

The worship service was literally a bloody mess, for which the stench of the smell of blood was aromatically dominating, sending off a very displeasing odor to the human sense of smell, as the animal sacrifices would have to be slaughtered outside of the tent of meeting, the blood would be drained and the carcase would be prepared for being burned on the altar for an offering to God.

But, simultaneously and mysteriously the blood was pleasing and acceptable in the nostrils of God. That will forever be beyond the comprehension of mere human understanding. We have to step into the realm of the spirit having repented and surrendered, dedicating our lives to worship the Lord in the beauty of holiness in order to even get to the beginning of intellectually reasoning to fathom the relationship between God and the original foundation of the blood.

The priest were required to mess up the site where worship would be taking place, and after the worship had ended they would also likewise be required to clean it up. Worship was indeed a job for the Levites and the High Priest. God was pleased for thousands of years until the blood of bullocks and of goats and of calves would no longer suffice the requirement of the Lord for the atonement of mankind.

God chose a sexually pure uncontaminated virgin who immaculately conceived of the Holy Ghost to avoid the sinfully contaminated blood of humanity to bring forth a child unfathered of any earthly man into the realm of humanity to wash those who would believe in Him and to save us all from the death of sin pronounced on humanity as a result of the curse of death which entered the blood of sinful humanity.

Jesus strategically came and stepped into the pitiful bloodline of all desperate humanity, offering Himself a ransom to buy back the spiritual purity of mankind through the shedding of His own blood. The unselfish gift of Christ's body and blood sent an explosive charge right in the heart of the Satanic takeover of the nature of mankind pronouncing an irrevocable notice of authority that heaven by way of Jesus Christ had finished the legal buy back of humanity, paid in full by the blood!

Although Jesus bled; and shed His own blood beginning at the garden of Gethsemane as He prayed until blood-like drops of sweat fell from His brow; when taken captive by the Romans, while the merciless beating began He bled as the Roman soldiers carried Him to Pontius Pilot to be Judged; He bled as they scourged and whipped

*Captured; Comprehensive; & Defined*

Him all night long with a cat of nine tails ripping chunks of flesh from His body, they plucked His beard and beat Him unrecognizably; (Isaiah 52:14) for a reference:

Even after all of that, they continued to whip Him up the hill as He carried His own cross, yet the fountain of His own blood continued to flow whereas that average human being would have already bled to death. Jesus takes on the pictographic exposition of the front entrance of the Tabernacle of worship where things were a bloody mess as they nailed the bloody disgrace of His body to a cross and hung Him there still alive to die for humanity even though they did not even believe that Jesus was dying for them.

The Blood of Jesus fell to the ground on Calvary's hill, thus tying up the loosened ends that were severed by the hands of Satan. If there is any question that Jesus came and died for all of humanity, I ask you again to reconsider the fact that Jesus' Blood fell to the ground where mankind was formed from the very beginning!

The fallen drops of blood to the ground should have signified to all of humanity that God in His own infinite wisdom and love, thought it necessary to revisit the work station from which man was formed and given life from the very beginning. We can never afford to forget that it was from the ground for which God through the blood gave life to humanity in the earth.

In Genesis chapter 4; the ground is rejected of the blood of the now murdered son of Adam, as even the blood of Abel finds discontentment and alienation in the ground and began to speak, crying out to the Father in Heaven over its lost condition after once again being poured out into the ground. However, as Jesus Christ hangs on the cross; being Emanuel [*God the Creator*] in the flesh; His own blood finds redemption in the ground in eternal agreement to the atonement of mankind forever.

As I look more deeply into the crucifixion of Jesus, I see the captors of Jesus trying one thing after another in effect to hopefully extinguish the life of Christ, but He just would not die!

Here's Why: Jesus stepped into the realm of dying humanity; being Life! Just how do you kill life? Jesus told us; no man take my life, I will (I have to) lay it down! (St. John 10: 18) *emphasis added* Can you not understand that had they been successful at taking the life of Jesus that humanity as a whole would have fallen away simultaneously and ceased to live! Even they themselves who had taken the life of Christ would no longer be able to live; they would never know the consequencies of their own successful crucifixion.

Jesus' blood spattered into the eyes of one of the Roman soldiers while he gambled for the robe that Jesus wore; blood ran down the side of the cross until Jesus pronounced before the throne of God and to the foundation of the world; "IT IS FINISHED!!!" For some reason the soldiers which stood by from the sixth to the ninth hour of the execution as Jesus hung on the cross, thought the need to finish Him off! A soldier took a spear and thrusted it into Jesus' side!

Lastly, what was witnessed in finality was the coagulated blood running down His side from underneath the fifth rib, which was a message to the Roman soldiers and to the Jews and to all of those that stood by, that all had already been finished right before their very eyes although they had not been in control of the finishing end! Blood and water ran down the side of Jesus, blood for the atonement of mankind, water for the washing of the water of the word of God.

The signification was that the blood of Jesus had successfully washed the sins of everyone who would believe! The ultimate message being levied upon mankind was that the blood of Jesus had once again restored the life we once knew in Adam, whereas we would fellowship in relationship with the Father! All on the premise of the blood!

My friend; are you washed in the blood of the Lamb of God? If not; come and be bathed and totally washed from your sins in the blood of Jesus; repent and know that you are now spiritually clean through the word of God. The peace of God which passeth all understanding will infiltrate your once guilty mind and set you free from the bondage of sin and of self in your natural body.

You have lived without Jesus Christ in your life; but, it is for certain that you can't die without Him!... Join me and plead the blood of Jesus over you and all that concerns you. Now!!!

# Chapter Four

# POWER OF RECOGNITION

*Now it came to pass in the Thirtieth year, in the fourth month, in the fifth day of the month, as I was among the captives by the river Che'bar, that the heavens were opened, and I saw visions of God. In the fifth day of the month, which was the fifth year of king Je-hoi'a-chin's captivity, The word of the Lord came expressly unto Ezekiel the priest, the son of Bu'zi, in the land of the Chalde'ans by the river Che'bar; and the hand of the Lord was there upon him*
.                           **Ezekiel 1:1-3**

## Knowing Your Source

As we move about the daily regimen of our individual lives, it is very necessary to have the power of God flowing through our beings. Everybody that I have come into contact with have exemplified a desire of some sort to be powerful in one way or another. Sometimes unimaginable efforts are employed to assure that the power sought will definitely be awarded to them. The same thing that it took to get whatever you wanted, it takes that same thing and even more to keep it!

Disrespect of self and of others just to be recognized as the one having the more powerful position of authority, people run right over one another like a steamroller, pulling each other down like crabs trying to get out of a bucket. They'd wedge themselves so deeply into the anticipation of acquiring the more powerful position of higher pay that they never appear to realize that they had already gotten what they wanted.

Misinformation, about power and the source that it flows from is even more detrimental to any power seeking individual. It is one thing to maintain the acquirable attractiveness about yourself, but it is altogether a totally different thing to keep pulling at a particular endowment simply because you have not recognized that you had indeed acquired the proper porfile requirement! Such self maintenace and even negligent failure to focus on self may leave you feeling as if you are of your own self, the source of the power that empowered you!

Many have confused the actual illumination of the light-bulb with the power source that caused the illumination. No matter how brightly a bulb may have been built to project, producing very bright light; the bulb may be capable of receiving very high voltages of wattage in power; the illumination is only the benefit of the source of power that produced the ability for the light to shine from the illuminated bulb.

A bulb will never become its own source for giving light, else all of the aisles in the stores would all be lit-up like the 4$^{th}$ of July, or Christmas. The light switch located on the wall is also likewise not the source of the power; its total function as a switch for the lights is reliant upon the flow of power to the light switch on the wall. Anything that obstructs or hinders the power from successfully flowing to the switch will not only blow the functionality of the switch, but, the lights will also fail to illuminate and to give off light.

The the power source that actually illuminates the light bulb has so many other functions and purposes. It is therefore arrogance to feel that we have come into the total knowledge of the power just because we have been made aware of one of its functions, or maybe even a few of its functions.

We often hear of and are totally overwhelmed about the wonders of the world whenever we personally come in contact with them. We should be as equally overwhelmed whenever we come in contact with the wonders that makes living possible for us in these modernized times. Electricity is a powerful wonder in our lives necessary for our wellbeing, but it is also dangerously destructive when mishandled.

As it relates to the very necessary element of electrical power, the operating rooms of our hospitals are definitely a host of surgical and medical wonder. If a person is blessed to remain alive after coming into contact with electricity they will usually end up in the operating room of the hospital, for which they will never forget. On the other hand, an electrical shock treatment could be administered to revive a heart patient whose heart may have stopped beating?

The ability to recognize is lodged within the power of recall, located within the logic of every individual's thinking capacitor. This ability puts every individual at square one as it relates to being equipped to even attach a name or a face to that which has presented itself to them as power. Apparently, many have leaped out of the starting blocks running with only what they thought might have been a powerful endowment, only to collide with the disaster of the reality in a head-on confrontation of truly being powerless!

Nobody; without having been initially acquainted from the stand point of being introduced to have the experience allowing them to become knowledgeable could ever say that they recognized anything, anyone, or even any situation.

There are several definitive words substanciated beneath the word recognize to establish foundational relevance enabling the authoritive resounding resonance; thus giving credence to a stated fact. To say; that you recognize; states, that you have the given precedence to independently execute the measure of a cognitive aptitude hidden within to reasonably draw the picture in your own mind from your memory to perceive.

One of the more defining syllables of this word is the pre-fix re: *which means to do again, or to repeat.* One of the greater deceptions of this generation lies within the desire to redo that which has never been done initially, by them. This deception is often realized whenever people put forth the perception that they presently know and recognize the presence of the Lord Jesus Christ with whom they have never been personally acquainted.

In all fairness, they may remember a spirited atmosphere, whereas the people of that particular event and time might have behaved themselves as if to have been in the presence of the Lord; Leaving the others to feel as if they knew the presence of the Lord themselves from now on? Desiring, is a great part of getting to know the Lord, although it is often distantly faint in one's heart. But, it never subsidises for the truthful actuality of being faithfully acquainted with Him through repentence.

The very next part of the word, recognize; is the base root word cognize: *which is to take cognizance of; perceive; know.* To become acquainted is to put forth the act of being cognizant. In other words, it is the time when you actually become aware and mentally configure what has been presented to you for the purpose of retaining a mental image.

It might be beneficial to you if the word collect were added to your understanding of the meaning of the word cognizant. Collect: *is to gather together, or to bring together;* which is only part of what it actually means to be cognizant. It is extremely necessary to bring into alignment and into proper order those things that have been gathered into our minds.

Cognizance bespeaks of our mental acuity and it will show forth to others that we are in control of our own minds as we choose and follow after our choices. Often in our society, we hear of certain individuals who after having been arrested they are released from jail on their own recognizance.

They are competent to the realization that they are not being excused from the crime, and that they are not being set free to go on about their lives. Upon leaving the jailhouse they are aware that they are to stand trial for the crime committed and the possibility that they may have to return to jail if they are found guilty of committing the crime to which they have been accused.

Recognition is a very powerful word, in that everyone that is competent to realize that they have the ability to recognize should also be encouraged to believe that they are empowered to have, to know, and to be whatever they desire in this life. The only true way to recognize is to be able to remember.

## The Ignition of Cognition

We've all had the experience of seeing a lot of things in our lives, and instructively listening to information being taught to us that have been powerful enough to leave indelible impressions in the spirit of our minds. But, the problem with many people lies within their inability to mentally mark the detailed data impute of what they have seen or have been taught for the simple reason that most people are at play when in fact that ought to be seriously marking on the tablet in their minds.

Most people on an average have not at all learned how to come out of the playgrounds of their minds; they're consistently on the merry-go-round; or they're in the party mode at even the most seriousness of times. There is far too greater allowance for recreational thinking, intentionally avoiding the seriousness of building our mental strength; or rather flexing our mental muscle! It is absolutely of no benefit to see and to learn a plethora of things if you never really intend remember anything that you've acquired.

God in His infinite wisdom; He knows that you and I, won't just necessarily remember things that will be of importance to us in the future on a whim, at every waking moment of our lives for no reason at all. There has to be a reason for remembering the different things that have crossed our paths. Things of situational and happenstancial experiences need to be meaningful if ever they are

*Captured; Comprehensive; & Defined*

to be regarded as substance to us, else we think of things as just a lot of stuff that came our way for any number of unknown reasons!

A like attitude can be gleaned from the experiences of being stopped in the traffic by a patrol car to be cited for a traffic violation. While in traffic, a driver may feel that everything is in order, only to realize that the officer of the law has stopped them to enforce a law that had been violated. Whether we are aware or unaware of the broken law, the fact is that we will probably never forget the incidental experience of being stopped by the police.

The enforced law may have been thought of as being so miner to you that you felt that it was unnecessary to penalize you; or maybe you just didn't know that law existed! However, being stopped ignited remembering in the very spirit of your mind no matter how you might have responded to being cited.

The medical profession has got a method in the maternity ward for igniting the initial cognition necessary for later recognizing. I entered the delivery room for moral support with my wife to witness the birth of my three children. Those were very interesting and an unforgettable experiences from the beginning to the end.

I have quite fond memories of things that were approving to me, and of course I can remember things that I did not approve of at all so well that left me wanting to take a few matters into my own hands. I can say that I remember all of these things as if it were happening just yesterday being that the impact of it all was so great. Often as I look upon my children now that they have grown so big and tall, I'm reminded of their exciting beginnings and of course I have and will always recognize them as mine.

What I remembered most of those impacting experiences was the nurse placed the new born child into my arms even before they placed the child in the arms of their mother. That always blew my mind for years, because I felt at that time that the nurses were only attempting to advise me that the child was indeed mine, of which I knew that I was the father better than they did. I had no understanding of the delivery room manner in which they conducted themselves, even after it occurred over and over again.

After many years of going over those incidents in the delivery rooms, as my children grew and even became adults, the revelation came to me that that was the ignition or the igniting of both mine and the infant child's ability to recognize each other as parent and child for the rest of our natural lives.

Many times in our lives something has to trigger the ignition of cognition to start the fire of remembering in the spirit of our minds, else we would come in contact with many different things and people in our lives that may never have any meaning or they may lose any meaningful relevance to us as time progresses onward.

The actual ignition of cognition is to be cited as an initial experience. Whatever our experiences are, these are the things in our lives that we are most prone to recall and to never forget. You have to experience the presence of God; accepting Him as God; even if another spirit filled individual has to tell you that it is the presence of God that you are presently experiencing?

I guarantee you that once you have come into the presence of God as a personal experience and have been made aware of the fact that it is indeed God's presence, you will never forget it for the rest of your life. Plain old common sense should allow you to agree with the fact that you don't easily forget experiences whether they are good or no good at all.

Experiences are like extended lighting elements in a light fixture or a bulb that gives more light to the illumination of remembering in the mind's eye. Whenever you look back over an incident the light of remembering seems to be turned on over that particular experience allowing it to be replayed in the spirit of your mind. Depending on the experience, it may appear as if the re-run of a motion picture has been placed on a movie screen.

### Did You Recognize or Realize?

Every individual should come to the point of realizing everything that there is to know in their own atmospheric surroundings. It is far greater to recognize the things of your own surroundings because it bespeaks of the fact of your awareness and connection to your own surroundings. But, it is equally as important firstly to come to the point of realization for yourself so that you can always be sure that you know what it is that you believe yourself to recognize to be your own surroundings.

It is detrimental to the spiritual welfare of any individual for them to refuse to be taught or to be informed by another individual that might already know. These latter generations are dead set against anyone instructing them in the way of the Lord, they have been led to believe often times through other secular sources that they can get all that they need from knowing the Lord on their own without a preacher or a teacher.

It is factual that absolutely no one can teach you to experience, though they may be equipped to lead you in how to go about getting the experiences that you may need to succeed in life. But, they can teach you how to realize when you will have had the different experiences that would have come your way. Sometimes you can come to know of the type of experience that you may have had and the knowledge to handle the experience through listening to others that have had the experience before you.

Getting acquainted is only the initial step of truly experiencing God; the next step is accepting Jesus as Lord and Savior. The writing of the gospel book of St. John will show you how to handle the experience with the presence of God as Jesus did Himself. You'll need to know how to handle that very same knowledgeable acquisition.

Whenever an individual come to know the Lord; they will have come into a wealth of knowledge so great that it has the power to cancel out any prior knowledgeable input. The knowledge that we have acquired for living is at best in need for the wisdom of God to be applied to it.

Without God's wisdom, the places of our spirit and intellect where we store knowledge becomes like a closet storage space or a warehouse filled with a lot of stuff on the shelf. Sometimes it never becomes useful to us for the lack of being able to realize the necessary implication for the knowledge application.

This is how so many people have been allowed to meander in and throughout the church aimlessly wandering hopeless soon to become doubters; the reservoir of their understanding has been relatively emptied out, and they are in great need for a knowledgeable understanding of the newness of a life in Christ Jesus to be poured into them quickly.

# Chapter Five

# GUILTY

# JUSTICE ✶ ✶

*Dare any of you, having a matter against another, go to the law before the unjust, and not before the saints? Do ye not know that the saints shall judge the world? And if the world shall be judged by you, are ye unworthy to judge the smallest matters? Know ye not that we shall judge angels? How much more things that pertain to this life? If then ye have judgments of things pertaining to this life, set them to them to judge who are least esteemed in the church. I speak to your shame. Is it so, that there is not a wise man among you? No, not one that shall be able to judge between his brethren? But brother goeth to law with brother, and that before the unbelievers.*

**Corinthians 6:1-6**

For all have sinned and come short of the glory of God
**Romans 3:23**

Speak not evil one of another, brethren. He that speaketh evil of his brother, and judgeth his brother, speaketh evil of the law, and judgeth the law: but if thou judge the law, thou art not a doer of the law, but a judge. There is one lawgiver, who is able to save and to destroy: who art thou that judgest another? **James 4:11-12**

### Guilty? : Me; Or, We?**

We are definitely proud of being saved in the body of Christ! We are often so proud, that we lose sight of the fact that we were not always saved and washed in the blood of Jesus! Such pride has kept many from being compassionate towards those who are still in need of being saved, and it has certainly desensitized many from being able to restore another individual in the faith who falls just short of being as holy as they ought to be. Those that sin; again!

The people of the church have often become so hypocritical discussing the shortcomings of others, especially when they themselves may have been guilty of the very same infraction since they believed! People don't know that you might have been a participator in the sinful affairs of the person that you are all discussing.

Too many of the people are determined to look good in the eyes of other people that attend the church, they really don't mind lending a helping hand to destroy the image of another person. They don't mind pulling another person down in order to lift themselves up in the eyes of someone else that they may be trying to impress. Many people of the church have been led to believe that they are indeed okay if they are guilty of an offense, just as long as no one else knows about it!

The intended purpose of salvation, was never for the sake of those of us who have indeed been born-again, to ultimately look the part of a saint; which many people of the church have erroneously favored; but God intended that we would be changed from the inside out! The purpose for salvation is always to change us from a life of sin and shame, to a life of righteousness and peace in the Lord Jesus Christ.

So many of the young people that I came up with in the C.O.G.I.C. church, they left the church as soon as they were adult enough to do their own thing. Many of the elders that are now resting in their graves, they placed image over and above that of character and actually being saved! Many of the young people of the church were taught that if they were not yet saved, that they had better look and act as if they were indeed saved; other people were looking at them!

Our parents and the elders brought us to church, and taught us to pray and to study the bible: nothing at all wrong with any of that! But, they forced many of the young people to adhere to the dress codes of the church, and they hardly allowed them to associate with the other young people of the communities except for being at school with them. They had to behave themselves as if they were already saved on the inside, and convinced in their own minds.

The truth is that they were being convicted by somebody else's mind? They were often inadvertently forbidden to think with their own minds, to make their own decisions to be saved. As a result, they were not influenced to come into the church to be the next leaders of the church, many of them; they were driven away from what had been painted to them as a boring and legalistic life.

As we have emerged to now be the adults of the church, we have to admit that many of the things that might have been suggested to us in Sunday School, and the training sessions of the church to be un-enjoyable, and undesirable to us, that as we matured to exercise our abilities to choose for ourselves as real life human beings, many of those things were indeed pleasurable. Sin feels good; and it brings that since of forbidden pleasure that we were never to experience or to ever know.

How many people do you think would remain in sin, if sin really had nothing to offer at all, as many of the people of the church have been taught at one time or another; though it may be only momentary medicating pleasure?

The truth is that what sin has indeed to offer

to us ultimately, is not at all what we really want! Whatever you feel at the moment as a result of the sin that you are in is not the reward that you are going to get! Forbidden sexual pleasure between two people of the opposite sex, never told anyone, while they were in the midst of having that sexual experience that they would get a baby as result of their well participated pleasure of sin! You might have gotten what you asked for at the moment, but you didn't ask for what you ultimately got!

Lots of people in the church were pressured into hypocrisy, in that they had to meet a certain criterion before they would be allowed to be a vital part of the ministry. So, instead of knowing the people for who they truly were, they relied on what they thought they witnessed in the lives of these people around the church, to determine whether they were justifiable to serve the ministry of the church.

At the church; is not where you are going to be able to tell whether or not a person may be living according to the word of God! People that may attend the services at the church on a regular basis are often dubbed as faithful children of the Lord. Search the scripture, and you will find that your church attendance is not what is going to be of the most important issue to answer to when we come before the Lord in judgment.

Of the greater mistakes made in and around the church, has been making the assumption that the people that are most available to the worship services of the church, that they are truly dedicated to the Lord, and definitely saved! People know how to look the part, and they know how to step up to the occasion to be presented as a favorable choice to carry out a particular task in the church that would be more preferable for one that has truly been changed in Jesus Christ.

People by the scores have learned how to put on church, rather than how to be the church in this perverse generation of people. As a result, the on looking populous of the surrounding communities in our societies, have scanned the churches noting that the same people that are often to the left of what is expected from members of the local churches, are the same people who forefront the ministries of the churches, also!

We have to admit that just because we have become members of the church, that those who sin frequently without conviction or desire of reframe, that they have often made it to the helm of the leadership in our own circle of Christianity.

### They're Good People??*

What too many of the people of the church have not realized is that we are not trying to get people to be good; our purpose is to get them to be saved! Around the church, it has become a common occurrence, for the leadership and the more respected members of the church to go to bat for certain persons of interest who are not yet saved and changed, when they had been cited for their own adamant sinful behavior, even though they were frequently in and around the church for services.

**People will often say;** *"they are good people, with a good heart, so they should be left alone, and allowed to participate in church affairs."* I must admit that I, myself have also been guilty of fighting on the behalf of some that I felt that all they need was a little more time to get themselves together and to make the right choice to receive Christ. Erroneous teachers have led us to believe that it actually takes longer for some to come to their senses, than it actually takes for others.

As a result, on the premises of good intentions, we allow certain people to flirt with the decision of salvation of their own souls, even in the presence of the savior. While it is their own choice to make, it's our responsibility to encourage them and never to enable them to remain in sin not even a moment longer than they had already.

We teach that life is uncertain, but that death is for sure! Even in respect of the truthful reality of that statement, we will elevate good behavior over and above that of being saved and washed in the blood of the Lamb! Some people are really dumb founded, and confused, as to why it is that they have to behave themselves and why it is that the people that are in the church participating every time the church doors are open have to be saved?

This is so, because they see these people on their jobs, in the neighborhood, and God knows that they see them everywhere else they go behaving as if there had never been any altering effect of the church in their lives.

So whenever confronted by the true Christians of the church, they begin immediately to argue that they are good people, and they live better than certain people that they can point out as a credible witness, of which sometimes that person that has been identified as an imposture to the church has been the pastor! They believe that if the pastor can't be held accountable for their behavior away from the church, then why should they be held accountable?

The struggle with sin in the first place, is the fact that people want to do it! It takes the power of the Holy Ghost to take away the desire from us to sin on a daily basis. Anyone who tells you that they don't want to do that, which God has forbidden, can't possibly be living in the flesh, with their feet on the earth. They have left the presence of this world! I say this because, as we are educated through the word of God about the pleasures of sin, we learn that the pleasure of sin in and of itself is not even the focus. What we learn to focus on is the consequences of our decisions to indulge ourselves in sinful practices, on a daily basis.

Good people do a lot of bad things, and they make a lot of bad choices, and they definitely create a lot of detrimental mistakes! Whether or not people are willing to admit to their mistakes and to their refusal to be the very best that they could ever be on their own, doesn't make it to be that they are indeed free of human frailties. How good are you really, when you don't even have the mind to take responsibility for yourself, to admit to the mistakes and the sins that you have committed?

Everything that God ever made was good, and that even includes you! But, good alone just won't do, because good in the earth is often subject to go bad! No matter how good you have dubbed yourself to be, you will never be as good as God! And the problem with humanity is the fact that we need to be as good as God is, right here in the earth where we live among other people, but it takes God to make us that good! We can't do it alone of ourselves!

How many times have we watched a news report of how that a good person has gone badly? And of course those things that are good to us and to humanity, we don't even want to begin to discuss how it is that they are no longer considered to be good for us now that we have been saved!

We have just recently gone through the tomato scare of the century; (2009). We here in America, we didn't even know just how important tomatoes were to the welfare of our daily consumption, until we were advised not to eat any tomatoes! Most every restaurant took tomatoes off of their menus, removed them from salads, deleted them from sandwiches, of which it was the tomato that actually made the sandwich delectable. A good thing went bad!

One of the nation's top, and most respected Bishops in the clergy, the right reverend Bishop Earl Paulk, though he had the power of influence by way of his own good self presentation; in that he had a congregation in excess of thousands, allowed his own mega ministry to come crashing down to the ground as a result of bad behavior during his tenure as a good leader. A good man, according to his record of many years of ministry, had done bad things in secrete that would find its way out from underneath the covers to the forefront of the headlines in the national media.

Never, in my own history as a young man of the church, had there been a man that preached to us the Holy Ghost like Jimmy Swaggart, of Baton Rouge, La. Many lives were changed, and spiritually transformed as a result of the powerful messages that he brought to the airways. But it was a bad thing, not the good things that he did, that brought him down from the limelight and the rightful place of reverence in the heart of the people. Yet even he was a good man!

Ever since the fall of man, man all alone of himself, through his own ignorance and stupidity, have made the attempt to prove even to God and to mere-men all over the earth, just how good he can be; though he has proven over and over again just how mistake prone, how vulnerable, how bad and sinfully wicked he really is without God! We must begin thinking God, and not just thinking how good we think some people are around the church.

## Guilty; Just -Us**

I often wondered why the media would have frenzy, whenever one of the good men of the faith would fall, though they would indeed fall hard. You might attest to what I am about to say; you know in the eyes of the sinful and the unbelieving, we that openly confessed to have been washed in the blood of the Lamb, and changed from our own sinful and evil ways, they who are of the world who could not even begin to fathom the reality of such spiritual transformations, ultimately believe that we should never be found guilty of any gross negligent behavior ever again. And to a certain degree they are right!

Here is what I have actually really come to know; relative to the sinner and the unbeliever, as it relates to the relationship that we have with our God! They truly envy us with extreme jealousy for having found the reality of the very thing that they themselves do not even know where to even begin a search! We have found that which gives us the greatest since of peace and tranquility, alleviating the need for a stiff drink or a drug of choice to aid us in escaping the plaguing realities of the confronting crises in our lives.

Our plight as blood washed believers, is that we often fail to realize that we had only gotten to the safety of salvation of the Lord before the other sinners who choose still to remain in the middle of their own chosen playpens of sin. Being saved never means that we are actually better that anyone else, but it does always bespeak of the fact that we are now better off having the Lord in the our lives, gauging the behavior of our lives according to the word of God, temporing us even when the unfavorable things of living show up in our lives.

It might appear that the grace of God may have gotten to us first, but don't get it twisted, our forthcoming to be saved whenever we did doesn't pose any threats to the imminent flow of God's grace for those who are still in need of the saving grace of God. Many saved people need to understand that they did not absorb all of the grace, no matter of how sinful they might have been before being saved, and just because others did not come to the Lord at the same time that you did does not prevent them from coming on afterwards.

The grace of God is available to all; but, what makes the difference is how responsive we are to the saving grace of God. It is not really that it takes some longer to come to the Lord to be saved than it actually takes others, it is however, that others are not necessarily readily as responsive and believing to take advantage of the saving opportunity in the grace of God.

People believe that whatever doesn't kill you will only make you stronger! And guess what; they're right! But, what it is that they have not taken into consideration is the fact that death in and of itself in many instances, is a process; it may be slow, but it is definitely for sure, even as the possibilities for death get stronger, the longer it is that you remain in sin!

The average person is not even equipped to examine the areas of their own lives that are affected as a result of their own sinful choices. When revealed, many are not very pleased with how strong they are in their own stubborn will to sin against the will of God, and they have discovered that they cannot even control the deepened propensity for sin.

So while they take the time to continue on in their own way, they are often blinded to the fact that time is running out! The bible didn't lie about Jesus coming back for a church without a spot or a wrinkle, as many have begun to feel since the Lord has not come back as of yet, and even since they first began to hear this message, whether they believed it or not!

Just because He hasn't got here as of yet, doesn't mean that He isn't coming! He'll be here when we least expect for Him to show up! We have to be prepared for His arrival, not just hanging around the church thinking about making the decision to one day invite Christ to come into our heart, of which by the way, the profession of Christ through our faith, it does ultimately prepare us for His imminent return. We'll be ready!

Some people stay away from the church because they believe that it gives them an alibi and excuse for never coming out of sin? They believe that only the people of the church are going to be judged according the bible, because we have surrendered to the power of the scriptures to govern our daily lives. Even people that are in regular attendance to the church, refuse to respond to the word of God at times, feeling that their unresponsiveness to the present spoken word of the bible alleviates their responsibility to that particular word of command.

I hear more and more people admonishing others to just go ahead and live their lives to the fullest, regretting nothing that they will have done as a result of living according to their own, grown up choices! They say that life in and of itself; is too short not to experience everything that had ever been desired. As a result of this type of living philosophy, many people are determined not to ever feel guilty about anything that they had ever done. They feel that whatever the circumstantial outcomes, as result of the behavior patterns that lead to destruction, were just supposed to be that way! Oh Well!

Most of these same people feel that we are stupid and ridiculous for allowing the church and the bible to make us feel guilty, or rather to give an account for living the way that we wanted to, no matter who disagrees with our choice of living?

The world sees that we are not only dealing with parishioners who attend the worship services of the church that are still guilty of sinning, but that we are also dealing with guilty leadership who are responsible for showing us the way of salvation through Christ Jesus our Lord, who are not themselves finished with living in sin. Many are the same leaders that are admonishing the churches and the world of the penalties of sinning.

We will judge the world according to the word of God, but only those that are truly blood washed in the blood of Jesus will be on God's panel of judges. Those who live sinful without seeking repentence will receive their just reward and due judgment; but my friend where do you stand right now in this present world while you put a difference in the church and of those who never attend a church?

# Chapter Six

# A REPROBATE MIND

*And likewise also the men, leaving the natural use of the woman, burned in their lust one toward another; men with men working that which is unseemly, and receiving in themselves that recompense of their error which was meet. And even as they did not like to retain God in their knowledge, God gave them over to a reprobate mind, to do those things which are not convenient,* **Romans 1:27-28**

## Reprobate Refined

1. Probate-the legal certification of the validity of a <u>will</u>
2. Pro-substituting for, acting in place of; A. rudimentary-existing at an elementary or basic level; developing-in an early or partially developed stage; undeveloped-biology not fully developed; biology in an embryonic state; B. precursor; somebody or something that comes before, and is often considered to lead to the development of another person or thing;
3. Probe-Investigation-a thorough investigation, often into illegal or suspicious activities; to conduct a thorough investigation of something
4. Probable-likely-likely to exist, occur, or be true, although evidence is insufficient to prove or predict it; Likely Choice-somebody or something that is likely to be chosen for something or is likely to do something
5. Repro-same as reproduction or proof
6. Bate-to beat the wings wildly or impatiently in an attempt to fly off a perch or a falconer's fist when still attached by a leash

## Understanding Defined

The pronouncement of a reprobate; have been avoided as of late, when calling out certain persons, whose behavior mirrored that of the scripture's purported descriptive activity of their own chosen improper gender manifestations.(Romans 1:19-28) Many men and women alike of this country in and around the local churches have taken on trans-gender behavior, and even cross-dressing as if even they might be able to amask their true gender to the onlookers of the body of Christ; they fail to acknowledge the lies manifested in their chosen behavior.

The leadership have too often strayed from formidably classifying; openly marking this ungodly behavior as such that it is truly, whether it is by reason that they themselves are also secretly alike in character to those who are effeminate in the spirit of their character or simply they lack the integrity of a truly anointed leader of God. Many; may not otherwise be in the condition of being reprobate; transfixed into the damnable state of being eternally Hell bound would the leaders only open their mouths and speak the truth of God's word to set those captives free!

The affixed attitude of those who have truly believed in the demonic lie relative to same sex attraction is often rattlesnake like in temperament due to the fact that they have erected walls of resistance to prevent others from persuading them to rethink their behavior. The shell like attitude of covering to which many of them have constructed about themselves is rather impenetrable like that of the tough thick scales of an Alligator or Crocodile; only the spirit of the Lord can penetrate the self-righteous covering if the person underneath allows Him to.

We have often made the mistake of assigning demon spirits in totality as being the root cause of this behavior suggesting that the persons laden with this sinful vise, that they perhaps cannot help themselves out of the condition, as many of them have confessed that they had tried to change? However; being pronounced as reprobate suggests to us that are willing to hear what the spirit of the Lord and the word says that God recognizes the individuals themselves as the responsible culprits for their own sexually deviant lifestyles.

Satan and all demon spirits have already been sentenced eternally for their sinfully wicked behavior; it is rather twisted and ignorant to believe that God is going to let you off the hook for your own willful sinful participation to dishonor your body as if God didn't give it to you, unless you repent and turn from your own wicked ways of thinking and doing. The detriment of many people who frequent the church is in the fact they don't believe that God really means whatever He has said concerning our behavior. They think that they are secretly bloodwashed because they attend the church.

For the very same reasons of hesitation to believe that God means whatever He says to us about us is also the underlying reasons that many people fail to adhere to the call of God on their individual lives. So many people just go ahead and live as sinful and as wicked as they can be as long as they can say that they have enjoyed the lifestyle they chose to live. So whenever they do hear the voice of the Lord calling them to surrender their lives to His will they have the nerve to cite their own past indiscretions to the Lord as if He didn't already know?

So as if to dull their ability to hear the voice of the Lord calling them anymore, people literally bury themselves deeply underneath the weight of sinfully wicked behavior. For a lack of teaching from the leadership of the churches many individuals who have purposefully wedged themselves deeper into sexual wickedness cannot focus their minds on the fact that God has a time of discard for which He will pronounce them as reprobate! No one can unsay whatever God has said concerning you!

Since the early 90's and at the entrance of this new Millennium we have often forgotten that sin pays wages? We will regret not haven repented for the sins we will have committed. Deception is on the increase to the point that people are determined to just go ahead and sin anyway; people now think to themselves that the consequences won't matter as long as they have enjoyed themselves!

Most of the leaders that I studied under would suggest to the congregation that no one could actually say when a person was indeed declared as reprobate in their minds, that only God would be the one to know of such a state in mind? I have lived to mature in the word of God and in the spirit to realize that studying the word and receiving revelation from the Lord would allow me to

*Captured; Comprehensive; & Defined*

know the characteristics whenever I would lay eyes upon such an individual.

For the past 30 years or better I have desired a true understanding of the meaning of being declared a reprobate, after reading the scripture all I knew was that that word would never describe me in character ever! Herein you will discover my research and study and hopefully you can appreciate what I have been given to share with the body of Christ worldwide.............

Lying just underneath the word "reprobate"; are six formidably conclusive and definitively comprehensive words to clearly retro-constitute in totality, what has been pronounced by God, on those who have chosen to practice without refrain, the self aggrandizement behavior of same-sex, sexual intercourse.

Is God unjust; or even unloving; having already defined and mandated what should be the proper sexual behavior of men and women alike, to pronounce such a judgment on those who have forged their own perverted ideological will over against the installed boundaries of partnering for the purpose of mating thus alleviating the power of reproduction?

People have been finding out since back at Sodom and Gamorrah, that doing whatever you want to do sexually to fulfill your own fantasies and to satisfy your own burning lustful curiosity with same-sex gender, family members, animals and beast; that it comes with undesirable penalties and painful consequences without a doubt!

God loves us all too much to allow us to do

our own thing knowing that it is going to cause us to live totally contrary to the written word of God without consequences. We answer to God; He does not answer to us, or even ask our permission before He requires us to live according to His word. Just because God judges the actions that we take unto ourselves, that doesn't mean that He doesn't love us with an everlasting love; He Loves Us.

The punishing judgment is relative to the chosen actions, the sinful deeds; whereas those who purposefully adhere to those deeds will likewise perish with the deeds should they be found in judgment still having the sinful spirit attached to them! God loves all sinners, but He must punish sin! [Refer to, i.e.; "ONCE BITTEN FOREVER, THE TREE OF KNOWLEDGE OF GOOD AND EVIL", WM. THOMPSON JR. COPYRIGHT 2009]....................

Such deviant sexual behavior is pointless and non-productive to the actual human cause. It is at best only an experimental exploration long since forbidden for humanity since the time of God's introduction of the woman Eve to the man Adam in the Garden of Eden. The atrocious behavioral attempts to suggest to the creator that there had been some sort of a mistake made at the point and time of gender establishment, also suggest failure to a God who can never fail!

Even though people have been determined to do their own thing, especially as it relates to sexual relationships, the pronouncement of a reprobate mind should show us that God is not in the dark as it relates to human behavior and neither is He going to just allow human beings to do as they please without suffering the consequences for their behavior.

> Know ye that the Lord He is God: it is He that hath made us, and not we ourselves; we are His people, and the sheep of His pasture. **Psalms 100:3;**
> The Lord is merciful and gracious, slow to anger, and plenteous in mercy. He will not always chide: neither will he keep his anger forever. He hath not dealt with us after our sins; nor rewarded us according to our iniquities. For as the heaven is high above the earth, so great is his mercy toward them that fear him. **Psalms 103:8-11**

Within the word itself we discover the immutable reasoning for which God has so forever detested same-sex behavior among the human race, assigning a sentence of affixitive permanence, as a result of one's determinate will to indulge them self knowing that it was indeed forbidden to do so from the beginning.

> Thou shalt not lie with mankind, as with womankind: it is abomination. **Leviticus 18:22**

God; being knowledgeable of the intended purpose of gender deference very wisely created opposites for the purpose of procreation, in that we as mankind would only be able to reproduce after our own kind in the earth, as equal opposites; a male and a female. The man and the woman is within the given nature of both the male and the female alike, but; however, neither male nor female can be produced without the sexual copulation simultaneously of both the man and the woman.

In other words, the man and the woman are within the seed of the man, but he has to place the seed inside the vagina of the woman, {not within the rectum of another man}; to produce the man and/or the woman which is indeed also inside of the woman as well. Female on female sexual encounters are so definitely unnecessary in that the woman does not have a seed to plant inside of another woman and neither has she been given the right sexual male organs for giving a seed. No two men or two women can ever at anytime produce the offspring male or female from their own sexually perverted encounter.

As we have indeed been given the benefit of our minds to aid us in making the necessary and proper choice decisions for living our lives daily, it has also been bewildering to realize the danger of having the control of our own minds choosing to ignore the laws of God, in that we are rendered responsible for the mind controlled choices that we have made which are indeed contrary to the written word and the definite will of God.

It has been biblically determined that sin begins with a thought; it is the unconsciously subverted thinking of mankind whereas people consistently ignore their own nagging conscience in the pit of their bellies telling them not to behave in such manners that will eventually cause them to regret their own choice of actions. Evil imaginations and corrupt communication have caused people to go deeper into the abominable acts of same-sex behavioral patterns of living.

## Self Centered Society

Of these latter generations, people have really begun to live out loud against the grain of negative associations to the sexually deviant perpetrators of the homosexual behavior in the church and the society whereas they are cited as unnaturally affectionate to the natural and the more common sexual behavior of the general populous. No matter how comfortable certain people become with living the homosexual lifestyle; their behavior will forever be detestable in the sight of God, as a lie is forever.

People now desire to express their own sexual appetites in and throughout their communities and their cities where they are most comfortable and familiar to the surrounding patterns of living. The more they feel that people know them for who they really are; they feel that it is of no consequence to change their lifestyle for any reason. The attitudes are more so to the tune of saying; "you knew what you were looking at when I first walked through the door." "Don't act surprised now!"

The position for the local pastors among the society has always been to eternally secure a right relationship with God through the sacrifice of Jesus Christ on Cavalry's cross on the hill of Golgotha. But, because preachers have become more commonly adaptable with the people in their original unacceptable state, they have been lulled into a more amicable stance of friendship with the people who really need to seek the Lord for a change in their lives.

The purpose of preaching in the churches has never been for advantageous opportunities to

*A Reprobate Mind*

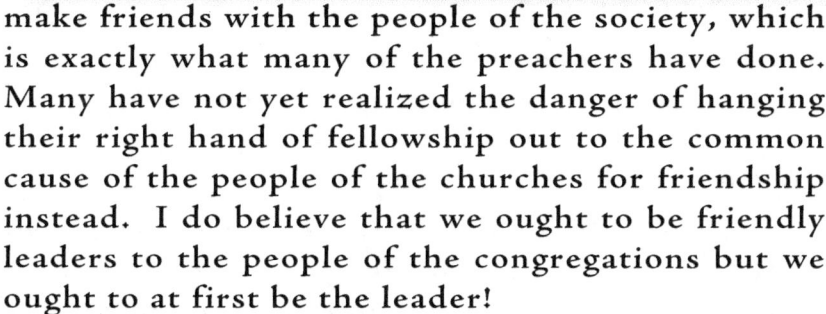

make friends with the people of the society, which is exactly what many of the preachers have done. Many have not yet realized the danger of hanging their right hand of fellowship out to the common cause of the people of the churches for friendship instead. I do believe that we ought to be friendly leaders to the people of the congregations but we ought to at first be the leader!

There is no reason that the preachers should be enemies with the people of the society who live for a more common cause of sin and self; only that is exactly what the people of the societies have become to the cause of Christ, they have become His enemies. For the simple reason that people are seriously offended with the idea of having to change from acting out according to their desired behavior, they don't want anything to do with the Lord.

People don't want to be bothered by any preaching even when the preacher can't be spotted as a phony and have been acknowledged as a true messenger from the Lord. Real true anointed preaching from the pulpits of any of the churches coupled with conviction from the heart of the messenger will prick the hearts of those who are perhaps living to the left of the required mandates of the word of God that are within an earshot to the message being spoken at the time.

Unless the messengers of the gospel walk in discernment as they intermingle with the people that attend their' churches, it may not always be easily detected just who it is that they are talking to and the level of hardening of the heart that any individual might have taken on as result of their own determinate will and indiscretion. A pretty smile or a handsome grin; does not make for the winning characteristics which calls for preachers to befriend the common people of the society, thus putting themselves in positions of neutrality to their own spoken messages.

An individual has to convince their own mind to accept the behavior to which their own bodies have been given to indulged. In one way or another we have all done things that we knew were wrong before we did them, but also note: we did not make a lifestyle out of those forbidden things. Thank God; there are still many of us here who have never been intrigued to try the homosexual perverted behavior, and don't mind letting you know that we are happy being who we are in our natural bodies as true men and women, male and female, boys and girls; and we whole heartedly believe the report of the Lord.

## Your Own Way In, No Way Out!

Isn't it bad enough that whenever we find ourselves in unfavorable situations that we often spend the balance of the time, if any time is spent in the experience, looking for the way out of it? Rationally thinking people don't want to spend their lives in misery or in miserable situations, without a solution to rectify things and to put us back into restored places of living according to the normal state that we were in before things got out of whack.

According to the experiences that others have reported in the media, in the churches and in documentary films or talk shows over the past years, those who live the sexually perverted lifestyles, usually live in misery and separation ousted from the common fellowship of the general populous of the community. You will often find many of them to be very angry and short fused, ready to fight at the drop of a hat, as a result of the pain that is alive within them.

Their own concept of normal has been so rejected by the naturally normal people of the society that they are infuriated and totally disgusted that people won't see normal as they themselves see it. What it is that they often fail to realize is the fact that it is God that have locked them inside of themselves to be the sexually deviant individuals in whom they have chosen to be? And now they don't even have a mind to even consider changing their way of living, they're set into their own way!

Most things that we get ourselves into we are usually able to get ourselves out of those things, as long as they are things in the natural realm and within our grasp to manipulate the circumstances. Though we may deal with the embarrassment of having been found in the middle of things that we should have never been found, still we are able to remove our selves.

We often prayed very diligently that the Lord would not allow us to remain in the situations that we had gotten ourselves into, and the Lord faithfully delivered us out of those things. Many times in our ignorance and sin we even challenged the Lord to free us, but only because of the fact that God is God; and because He searches the motives and the intent of our hearts, He had mercy on us, knowing that we could not even free ourselves from the bondage of the willful repetitive vice of the things that we had gotten into.

But, now the question becomes; just how often do we believe that God is going to continue to get us out of the mess that we have chosen to make out of our lives? Even when the mess has been a sexual mess God can and will get you out of it if you will determine to stay out of it!

When you have found yourself profiled and stamped as a reprobate true to the form in the written word of God, the fact is that it is of your own doing and personal behavioral choices; you have gotten your own self into a situation to which there is no way out for you!

The prescription for the reprobate description, in the word of God, is Jesus Christ! His own sacrificial offering on the cross for our sins is the overall remedy for the sinful "can't-help-it" of our flesh, whereas people are consistently telling God that they can't help but to commit sin! Some people sin until they have entered into abominable acts against God, whereas their sins have begun to stink in the nostrils of God like the rotting decayed flesh down in the grave.

The sins of same-sex behavior is so spiritually putrefied to the spirit of righteousness and of holiness having gone so far out of bounds to what would even be tolerated as common sinful human behavior, that God has no choice but to seal it up and to tie it off as a spiritual hazard to all of mankind. The purported spiritual behavior of mankind is endangered under the guise of the alternative gender base, as there is no spiritual provision of grace for such a rebellious act against the natural nature of mankind.

*A Reprobate Mind*

Even though Oprah Winfrey and other medical professionals have cited the gay lifestyle as a normal living option for having a mate, life partner, or even a spouse in these latter generations, allowing for people with twisted thought processes by the scores to come out of the closet with their decisions to live the gay lifestyle, God has forever declared it to be Unnatural! The fact is that it was rotten from the start, or even before you could even get started behaving in this unseemly manner of perverted sexual behavior.

Long since before now, those who have chosen the gay lifestyles have been found in the local churches playing on the instruments, singing in the choirs, ushering on the usher boards, and now they are even leading and pasturing many of the churches openly as members of the gay communities. Just about 25 years ago the gay community's had their own churches, whereas they would not even dare to attempt to take the helm of the previously organized Christian churches knowing that their behavior as a man or a woman was totally to the left; according to the word of God.

But because they were able to expose those members of the clergy that were "quote-un-quote" under cover, living as a hypocrite and a fake because they were also passively gay or bi-sexual in their behavior, they were cited as "down-low"; the other more aggressive gays began to migrate back into the fellowship of the churches undeterred by the general populous having carnal knowledge of the very insidious secret indulgence of certain leaders in the churches.

We who are the leaders of the churches are

to advocate salvation and redemption to the people of the churches having been redeemed ourselves already. The following of the gay leaders of churches have increased to a dangerous rage to the point that many of the gays no longer even feel that they need to consider the word of God for their behavior, thus more rapidly entering into the state of being declared reprobate! Their behavior patternistic styles of living have attacked teachings of the bible which demands the churches adherence to the idea that people should flee such devilish lust; whereas, they have even turned the tide against the church's labeling them "Homophobic!"

Jesus said; "the very day that you hear my voice, harden not your hearts."

Too many people are living out loud in retaliation of having too much factual sinful information on other people in the churches! This attitude of hardening one's self in resistance to change opens the door to the entrance of the affixation of being determinately recognized as a reprobate. It's crazy to say that you are willing to go to hell simply because you know other people that are going to hell also; would you burn up in a house fire simply because someone else didn't get out of the fire in time?

My friend, a reprobate mine is definitely a reservation to hell, whereas alike the reprobate mind, hell has one way in, but no way out! To those who are indeed a reprobate in their minds, they will never be found seeking a way out of their behavior. They are often shaking their fist and pumping their chest to God, saying to Him that it's His fault that they are in the situations they

*A Reprobate Mind*

are in. They have even accused Jesus Christ of being one of them, suggesting that Jesus had also been a homosexual.

Misery loves company! They know that they are indeed miserable in every aspect of their lives, so rather than to change their ways, they have assigned to themselves to change the reverenced image of Christ to as many of the masses as will be willing to listen to their rhetoric. What it is that I have found to be the truth of those who have been declared to be a reprobate is that they will not receive the truth of the word of God. They are sold on the twisted lies of perversion and they are ever attempting to sell the lies to the youthful minds that are vulnerable enough to be swayed.

Reprobates; know that they are indeed headed for the pit of hell, and they are going to take as many to hell with them as possible. This is the reason that you and I alike have not been successful at reaching them by reason of their minds, you can talk until you actual begin to change colors but they are not going to get the picture that you are trying to convey to them. They are determined within themselves that they do not want to change their behavior which is what defines who they really are.

> For as many as are led by the spirit of God, they are the sons of God.   **Romans 8:14**

I know many people of the churches who felt that they would actually enter into the status of being a "super-saint" should they be successful at getting the gays to truly turn to the Lord and be saved. Some have been saved and truly changed, but it is not a frequent occurrence to witness members of the gay community to come before the Lord to be saved, set free from their perverted lifestyles, and healed from the emotional destruction and annihilation of their mental thought process.

Since God knows who the reprobates truly are, it would be very wise to seek the Lord before going after those of the gay community that are truly sold on the idea of a same-sex relationships, otherwise you are only being distracted from ministering to those that can hear you and receive the message that you bring to them, and turn from their wicked ways and be saved in Jesus Christ. Listen to the Lord and don't waist your time!

# Chapter Seven

# POWERFUL PREACHING

---

*For I am not ashamed of the gospel of Christ: for it is the power of God unto salvation to everyone that believeth; to the Jew first, and also to the Greek. How shall they call on Him in whom they have not believed? And how shall they believe in Him of whom they have not heard? And how shall they hear without a preacher? And how shall they preach, except they be sent? As it is written, how beautiful are the feet of them that preach the gospel of peace, and bring glad tidings of good things!*
**Romans 1: 16, 10: 14-15**
*For Christ sent me not to baptize, but to preach the gospel: not with wisdom of words, lest the cross of Christ should be made of none effect. For the preaching of the cross is to them that perish foolishness; but unto us which are saved it is the power of God.*
**I Corinthians 1:17-18**

And my speech and my preaching was not with enticing words of mans wisdom, but in demonstration of the spirit and of power: that your faith should not stand in the wisdom of men, but in the power of God.     **I Corinthians 2: 4-5**

### Real; True; Preachers

There is nothing in this world that I enjoy doing better than preaching the gospel of Jesus Christ. Nothing compares to the joy and the gladness that I experience whenever it had been acknowledged that people were enlightened and encouraged to change their thinking about the scripture, their behavior whenever they are away from the assembly of the believers having decided to turn their lives over to the Lord Jesus Christ to be saved, set free and delivered.

Growing up, whenever my friends fathers would ask me what I wanted to do when I grew up, spontaneously I would respond telling them that I wanted to be a preacher! I knew that I would preach the gospel at 3 years of age! I have been in the ministry of preaching the gospel for the past 30 years of my natural life.

My father was not very fond of the fact that I would tell people that I was going to be a preacher, whether they were people in the church, in the neighborhood, or at school. He'd asked my mother who was putting me up to say those things, and he would often say that he wanted me to stop saying that. But even as a child I was driven to preach the gospel.

In Sunday school and the other training sessions of the church for the youth, my ability to reasonably understand, to dissect and to maintain accurate knowledge of the scripture was often cited as remarkable for a child of my age at the time. I was often on top of the subject from a biblical standpoint whenever biblical topics were raised as a result of good bible instruction, and proper training from my parents.

Although I was trained and properly instructed to know the difference from right and wrong, I was determined to behave myself like the rest of the boys in the neighborhood and at school, as boys will be boys; I lived to learn that adolescent misbehavior and sinful activity comes natural. No excuses needed; responsibility to acknowledge my own misdeeds is enough to explain how my life at times often did not reflect as I grew older the true calling of God on my life. Any sinfully common behavior will obscure the actuality of the call of God in an individual's life.

In school, very seldom was I ever called by my name, from the third grade upwards even until now many people have referred to me effectionately as; "Brother Bill," and at times some still do. My point in fact is simply, many people recognized that I was driven as a believer of the gospel of Jesus Christ.

These things did not please my natural father in the least bit at all. Amazingly, three of my father's brothers and one of his sisters were also preachers of the gospel; my mother's father was also a renowned minister of the gospel and an author of several books; by the name of "Rev. Vol William McLawler" of Louisville, Kentucky.

My father himself, even though he had protested often whenever he would hear me speak of preaching, he left this world April 6, 2000, an anointed Holy Ghost filled preacher of the gospel of God. Amazingly, he loved to preach himself, and he loved preachers. My father and my mother began preaching, being full of the Holy Ghost about 6-8 years before I ever preached my first initial sermon to the churches.

Before he ever answered to the call of God on his life to preach, we could walk into a church and the pastor or the pulpit conductor would invite him to the pulpit to be with the preachers. Sometimes it infuriated him to be singled out as a preacher while he had never answered to the call; but all the while that he had spent fighting and running away from the will of God on his life, he knew of the call.

Such is the case of the greater balance of those who were called of God truly. Even though many theologians argue against the validity and the authenticity of the written accounts of the Prophet Jonah, looking into the lives of many preachers even of today, you will find many paralleled similarities. It's never been the common demeanor of those who have been called of God to run into the direction of obedience to God immediately, because of the bourden associated to being the messenger of the gospel.

The individuals that have been called of God that truly fear the Lord, they often find themselves apprehensive to failing God should they answer the call and begin to declare the truth of God's word. As I have shared with many ministers in my own life I have heard several different story accounts of how they went deeper into living in sin, feeling that supposedly God would even change His mind about using them in the ministry. But, God don't change His mind as it relates to our preordained purpose and our calling.

Some ended up in the penitentiary for long periods of time even until they told the Lord yes; that they would obey the call. Some ended up in the hospital on the brink of death hooked up to life support for weeks and months having many very spiritual visitations from the Lord and even Angels of the Lord admonishing them to obey the call of God. Believe it or not, some even ended up in the insane asylum fighting for their own sanity as a result of refusing to be; whom God said that they were before the foundation of the world.

The stories are countless, as some are even mind-boggling, the lengths that some people would go to avoid the God ordained purpose of their lives. You would be surprised to realize that many of the alcoholics and the drug addicts that are even addicted to crack cocaine and methamphetamine of all races of people, right today, are in the conditions that they are in simply for the fact that they have chosen to run away from God.

In my own opinion; it's takes an altered state of thinking to truly be called of God and know this for sure, and purposefully lead your own life in the opposite direction away from God in direct disobedience and defiance to the will of God. I am not suggesting to you that those who are standing in the stead of the leadership are impostures and those that are the extreme partiers are those that may be the real truly called of God. That's Crazy!

The messages from the more religiously mo-

*Captured; Comprehensive; & Defined*

tivated churches, often suggest to the parishioners that the calling may only come after an individual may have obtained more experience of life through sinning in the natural before they might ever be qualified to be used of God. If such were only truly the case, Jesus would never have been sinless and neither would those chosen Apostles who came before us had admonished those of us who would follow after them to live circumspectly and clean before God in holiness.

Many; that have never been called of God; are the pastors of the religiously organized churches across the denominational spectrums of the world, they attended a seminary to become a pastor or a professional minister of the churches. I heard a pastor say from the pulpit of his own church; men go to school to be Doctors and Lawyers, and all other professional individuals, why shouldn't people go to school to become a professional preacher?

Some have taken their own finances to construct church buildings, and began to operate their own brand of church from scratch, having never been raised or trained in the church, and had never been taught from the bible by anyone who had themselves been spirit-filled and knowledgeable of the scripture, being apt to teach. In retrospect, many who were in the church for the balance of their lives, have revolted against the teaching of the scriptures and have begun to teach in contrast to the actual message of the bible.

This information doesn't balance out the differences of the negatives and the positives that are ingrained into the ministry of preaching the gospel, only those that have been called of God are to be the defining factors of what constitutes real true ministry. The pros and the cons of the ministry are hurled our way from day to day at record breaking speeds of unexpectancy however the call of God itself creates a shield of protection to them that are truly obedient to the call.

Then of course those who have been called of God ought to have a relationship with God whereas they have been anointed and endowed to speak the word of God with true conviction so that they can see the lives of people affected through the message of the preached word. Through the process of choosing and appointing individuals to take the roles and the offices of the ministry who had never been called of God by their own admissions, the actual power and the true purpose of preaching has been compromised.

### The Testing of a Preacher!

Many of the reasons that we have the very visible and the publically acknowledged rifts in the ministry is relative to the fact that God knows how to divide the true preachers from those that are indeed false. Frequently from the pulpits of the none spiritual leaders of the churches, for the purpose of manipulating their need to influence the people under their leadership, the messages can be heard relative to false prophets; but it's now time that we raise the issue of the false preachers in the churches who have taken on the helm of the leadership roles.

Often those who have never been called have been deceptively lured into the pulpits on the falsehood of the ministry being a comfortable place to abide in the church, the community, and even in the realm of religion. Only those who have the mind to receive the word of God firstly and to apply it to their own lives can be cited as the true ministers of the gospel. Just because we may have a drive to tell everybody else what the Lord requires of us, that does not make one a true preacher of the gospel.

Oh, but, so many have walked away from the church and the ministry in grave disappointment and often even extensive public embarrassment! They are now walking around among their peers and their detractors with their reputations shattered like a broken piece of glass, their egos have been bruised beyond recognition, although they had never been broken in spirit before the Lord.

What appear to matter most to them since they have fallen in grave disappointment is the fact that they are being ridiculed by people who never could have ever truly believed in them in the first place because they were never called to be in the spiritual positions to which they so purposefully assumed on their own will, having many hidden agendas.

I have seen some elevated all of the way up to what we would refer to as the top of the Christian platforms as a pastor, and leader of the church community, only to be publically, sociably, religiously, and personally flattened like a pavement after a steam-roller had finished going over it.

Some were successful at seating thousands of people at one time or another, while having the wool pulled over the eyes of the people of the church. Even banks and lending institutions have been duped by them to the point that they have loaned them mass amounts of finances for building projects all on their ability to charismatically dialogue business jargon. It's true; your mouth can take you to high places many times where your character will not be able to sustain you! The sins of your falsehood will tell on you to those who are following your leadership, or at least it should.

> and be sure that your sins will find you out: **Numbers 32:23;**

And my friends; I want to admonish you to be assured that your "SENDS" will also find you out!!! There is a distinct difference as to where the Lord sends you and where it is that you choose to go! Jonah didn't want to go where the Lord was sending him.

As a result, we have been made aware of the turmoil and the devastation that he caused others as well as the anguish that he caused himself. I believe that the belly of the fish was synonymous to the belly of hell; which is the only place that a disobedient preacher, and/or a preaching imposture will find themselves in the end.

On the other hand, Abraham went where the Lord sent him even though he did not even know where he was going; he simply went out of obedience to the word of God. And to this very day we are the direct results of the blessing of Abraham, being redeemed from the curse of the law of sin and death. Abraham's obedience has brought about a far reaching effect to the body of the Christ, to the comprehensive perspective of being obedient to the will of God as a called out leader.

Powerful preaching can only really exude from a powerful preacher who is indeed true to their calling in their own character as they walk before the Lord! How powerful are you when you can't even stand behind the words that you have spoken out of your own mouth? Are you really that powerfully projected preacher when it is by your own intentions to walk contrary to the written and mandated word of God? Are you truly that called out vessel of the Lord when in fact your total motivation is keeping in step with the world and your own surrounding society?

I mean; are you that complacent that you are not moved to make a difference and to show forth the righteousness of Christ when the same society is comparing the ministry of the gospel to the outlandish lifestyles of the Pimp and the Hustler? Especially, when those same destructive finger pointing comparisons are targeting at you! You may not even care about what people have to say about you, but there are times that you ought to take a bit of concern for the sake of the people that are following you.

Carnal minded non-spiritual leaders of the churches often lean to the fact that Jesus sat down and even ate with the sinners; but don't get it twisted, He didn't sit there with them to become like them, it was the only, real true method of showing the love of God to the unlovely of the society. Therefore, the greater affect was actually levied upon them and not on Him! Believe me, His presence left a lasting impression on them, and unlike any of us He didn't have to shake off the influences of any of the people that He had been around.

What is it; that convinces you that you are a powerful preacher when there are clearly no visible differences to distinguish you from the very people that you are preaching to? I mean that you still frequent the popular Night Clubs, still indulging in alcoholic beverages, still smoking the most popular brand of cigarettes, cuss like a sailor, you cheat and are dishonest in every expression of your character. I know people who speak of drunken preachers, and how it is that they are able to preach in the pulpits though still intoxicated.

Those ministers, who have truly been called of God to preach the gospel, they can and will stand the true test of their character and their biblical convictions, on the strength of their surrenderance to the will of God and the covering of the blood of Jesus when in the face of adversity.

I am not speaking to the beginning novice of the ministry that just came into the realization of their calling, I'm speaking to those who have been in the pulpits for even more than twenty and thirty years purposefully leading the people of the churches astray through the terrible and ungodly examples of their own lifestyles and behavioral patterns. I admonish you to get out of the pulpits while you still can and be saved. You can never be established as right or even righteous while intentionally living wrong and operating out of the will of God for your life.

Being broke and poor are not qualities for being in the ministry like some have been led to believe, but as a minister, how do you teach others that the Lord can and will provide for them if they have never seen you go through anything?

You do know the message that you are sending to the people of the churches whenever you turn to Drug Dealers and street hustlers for money, or when you begin stealing from the church just to keep up a particular lifestyle. By all means, you need to quit gambling, telling the people in your congregation; "anyway the Lord bless me I'll be satisfied!" The greatest teaching of any minister will always be done through the examples of their own faithfulness to trust in the Lord, which is made evident through their actions and behavior.

As a minster of the gospel of Christ you need to consider the fact that the sickness in your own body may in fact be for a testimony of the power of God to heal; but just how in fact do you suppose that you will get the message over to the people of the church when you never seek the Lord through the exemplification of your faith, trusting the Lord to heal your body openly and publically before all of the people. Perhaps you are leading them to die with you rather than to live with and for Christ?

### Preaching That's Reaching!

The mind boggling, and often peace disturbing challenges that any minister will face once they have truly surrendered in dedication to the call of God are simply the fine tuning streams of power that discipline your ability to reach while preaching allowing God to transform, to charge, and to anoint you as the leader. Redirect your ministerial focus in such a manner that you will actually become a ladder of extension into the presence of God for the sake of the people, figuratively speaking!

The called, anointed preacher is spiritually

taller and can reach upwards into the higher realms of the spirit for the sake of handing down to the people of the churches, those things that have been truly ordained of God.

For this reason alone, we that are ministers must not only spend time perusing the pages of the scripture for another bible story to deliver as a lesson to the people of the churches, but it is imperative that we give ourselves to extensive prayer to the father who called us in the first place. There is a grave danger hidden underneath the ability to preach without maintaining a life of prayer and fasting before the Lord.

Once we have learned the true essence of preaching, and have understood its purpose among the people of the churches and the society, it takes prayer to maintain the understanding to which we have come to embrace. Prayer keeps us focused and main streamed along the fine lines of the endowed purpose for which we had been called initially. Over the years I have witnessed many who have lost sight of the purpose of preaching, as they strayed into areas that will never have anything to do with the saving of the souls of mankind.

It is sickening to my stomach the things that are attributed to being a successful preacher, while there is not much associated to successful preaching. "Quote un' Quote"; successful preachers are seen all over the television networks, and they are involved with the political agendas of the society, they are even known among the who's who of societies elitists; they are often cited among the "best of the best."

They may be known among the famous clothing and shoe stores, and they are recognized by name at the top of the line automobile dealerships. It is no secret that they live in the gated communities, whereas they have employed maids and butlers, for which "I really do not take offense to that." When a person has been blessed to live above the norm of society, it is a blessing to be able to abide in that level of comfortable living.

The fact is that they are known and recognized as the more successful preachers of our modern society, for which many of the younger ministers and those who were once dedicated to reaching the lost for Christ have been influenced to drop off from the reach to just preach.

For the sake of those who are now living relative to what we will refer to as comfortable, they did not just get there over night and many of them did not get there on a preacher's salary. I will not say that it is the fault of successful living preachers that the idealism of being successful in the ministry has been marred, as far as I can see the fault lies within the fact that too many have stepped forth taking the ministry as a career having never been called.

And for the sake of those who might have been called indeed, they lack teaching, having no experience of living to know what the Lord will do for those who are faithfully dedicated to walk through the hard places of the ministry first, and or even to know the meaning of living without, lacking the better things of life before being prospered by the hand of the Lord.

The truth is that you can never reach where you refuse to look! It's obvious that people are looking in the wrong directions for the knowledgeable scopes of reasoning that allow themselves' to progress in the ministry. They are looking to man and on the things they have acquired since they have been in the ministry, not realizing that many of those ministers have obtained their worldly possessions by means other than by and through the power and the will of God.

> If ye then be risen with Christ, seek those things which are above, where Christ sitteth on the right hand of God. Set your effection on things above, not on things on the earth.
>
> **Colossians 3:1-2**

Back in the 70's we use to sing a song which said; "Look to Jesus, He's the only one who can." It's so necessary that ministers are raised up in the church in the presence of the Lord, for the simple reason that they may be able to glean from the working power of God having been a witness of the hand of the Lord working things out in their own life firstly, and seeing God move in the lives of others. It is most necessary to know personally that God is real.

Although I may see that an individual is living high on the society by the standards of the people in the church anyway, the allowed wisdom of the Lord will suggest to me according to the word of God, that in due season and time, my ability to prosper and to live comfortably will come to me based on my own ability to wait on the Lord in patience holding to His unchanging hand.

My attitude has always been that if the Lord don't do it for me then I didn't want it anyway! Faith in God has never failed me! Right now, despite the fact that I had to live past many challenges and climb many high mountains just to get to where I am, I and my family are living rather nicely, and it will be Greater; Later!

I can remember as a young boy, the church singing; "No Cross; No Crown!" The message of these types of songs led us to believe that the trying of our faith was definitely of God. People are in despair desiring to live better than they are, or at least equal to their neighbors, not having a clue at all pertaining to what the other people have had to go through just to get what they have.

See it's easy to look into the lives of others and to determine that you want what they have. But, looking doesn't allow you to see the circumstances of life that the other people may be living under. For an instance; I trust in God for whatever I need; my neighbor could be selling drugs, playing the lottery, dancing at a strip club at night, prostituting, or some other type of an illegal scheme just to have the extra income needed to maintain their lifestyle.

## Stay Focused

Listen; get your eyes back over into your own yard and keep your face towards God. I celebrate with others over their stuff knowing that it's not mine! I may be glad for you, but I can and will wait for my own. I want my own blessings! God's blessings are hinged on our obedience to the will and to the word of God.

The late; "Dr. S.E. Mitchell" use to say that

"if preaching get me into trouble, preaching will get me out!" Powerful preaching will at times cost you in terms of the trouble that it may cause you; but that same powerful preaching of the gospel will also vendicate you, as result of the spirit of truth of the word of God that is backing you all of the way.

Three points and a poem does not constitute powerful preaching by any stretch of the imagination. Powerful preaching won't net you lots of friends who prefer to spend their casual time in your company. Powerful preaching is so resounding, that even after you will have left the pulpit and the sanctuary of the building, the spoken words of the message that you had just released to the people of God can still be heard in the atmosphere, ringing true like the liberty bell, at Philadelphia, Pennsylvania.

Powerful preaching produces words of messages that won't be silenced anytime soon! The judge on the bench will have to hear the power of preaching, even though they have been chosen, and voted in to levy judgment calls upon the lives of the people of society for a multiplicity of reasons. The physician and all medical professinals, the undertaker who prepares the preachers body for viewing when their work has been finished, likewise they all must hear the power of preaching to change their lives!

It's ordained of God; preaching is ingrained into the master plan of God for all of humanity to receive the salvation plan of God, for us all to be redeemed and realigned to the intended purpose for Humanity in the earth, as we were made for the glory of God, to worship Him in the beauty of holiness and truth.

I am of the opinion, finally; that powerful preaching is in and of itself, unfailing reaching! Somebody is going to be reached without fail. Only one person may come forth at the time of the message, but just as a seed that is sown into the earth's soil all alone of itself, there is no telling how many other souls will be reached as a result of the one who came forth to acknowledge God in Christ Jesus to be saved set free and delivered.

Come forth preacher, and don't cower down in the pulpit, or in the congregation of the people, say what the Lord tells you to say, and say it the way that God in the spirit is saying for you to say it. Powerful preachers never alter the things of God, because the power of our preaching is relative to our obedience to God, and actually nothing else.

Always trust in the Lord as your source and fear Him; your Goliath must also fall on the battlefield before all of their own supporters and conrads. God is the greatest power of all in the cosmos; so with that being said, the only thing to fear is fear!!

> God has not given us the spirit of fear but of power and of Love and of a sound mind.           **I Timothy 1:7**

# Chapter Eight

## "FIRE"

---

*And I looked, and, behold, a whirlwind came out of the north, a great cloud, and a fire infolding itself, and a brightness was about it, and out of the midst thereof as the colour of amber, out of the midst of the fire.* **Ezekiel 1:4**
*For our God is a consuming fire.*
**Hebrews 12:29**

## *Fire; No Accident!*

Approaching this particular topic of discussion, I realized just how unknowledgeable we really are about fire, being earthly. The average knowledge of fire is that it's hot; and to stay clear and free of its burning path. In other words; we know much more about what it does, how it feels, how to safely apply the usage of fire to our daily lives, and the sociable and methodical preventive applications to ensure that we never allow opportunities for the destructiveness of fire to take hold of us.

Many theories relative to the actuality of fire's origin, the exact extensive capabilities relative to the possible uses, destructibility, enhancements, and the innumerable benefits to mankind. Yet we are consistently challenged of truly being knowledgeable of the definitive actuality of what the flame of fire is!

What is the consistency of the little spark that makes it powerful enough to set everything a blaze? Tell me if you can; who invented the spark? Did you know that the very same thing in the little spark is in the ignited flame? When we can definitively comprehend the spark, that is the time of which we will come to the point of truly understanding the true essence of the flame; thus we know what fire is.........

I have come to understand that when the lightning flashes, it first creates a friction against the surface of whatever it is that it strikes up against causing a spark. The material surface must then be receptive to the spark allowing for the continuance of the excited strike, creating the flame which grows bigger and bigger the longer that it is allowed to remain without being extinguished.

A doust flame is first a burning flame before ever being met with the smothering blanket of water, of sand, or of anything large enough to cover the entire surface starving it of oxygen to continue burning. Wherever we see the smoke and the charred residue of anything that has burned, we know without a doubt that a fire had been there!

Of the greater mysteries beneath the surface of burning fires, lies the truthful evidence that whatever was, is no more! The fire has done away with it; this is the reason that fire is so often used in the disposal of many things, because we know that fire destroys matter; most times anyway!

Therefore; in my own analogy, it is not really the powerful percussion in the flash of lightning as it strikes the surface of whatever it hits, as it strikes everything with the same impactful power, but not everything is conducive to the excitement of fire. For an instance: all of the waters would be dried up and totally evaporated if the flames could exact upon the water.

The lightning flash being electrical; water itself is a major conductor of electricity; so the water and the lightning are sort of married to one another, in that the relationship between the two elements is unwavering at all times. However; the surfaces of most solid and flammable objects are conducive to carry the elecrical current or to be ignighted by the sparks caused by the friction from the striking lightning.

Water in most situations, can temper the

*Captured; Comprehensive; & Defined*

outrageous flames of fire when we are in need of regaining temporal control. On the other hand, when water itself, is not conducive to our healthful requirements, it is the usage of fire that renders the water beneficial to us, in terms of sterilization, heating the water temperature, cooking, and most definitely for the benefit of bathing.

Even though water can be adversely harmful to us, and extremely destructive in massive quantities, it is also imminently needed, normal, and necessary for our survival, livelihood and for recreational pleasure. God; having constructed our bodies 87% from water, in His infinite wisdom; He also made the water more available, in the since that water is a bit more user friendly to us.

The contrasting difference; yet the parallel association of water with that of fire, relative to the human welfare in the earth are both mind boggling, in that they can be equally destructive to human welfare, yet they are both major elements in the humanistic realm for the simple benefits of daily living.

We dive into large pools of water for the purposes of recreation, education, and even exercise. We take to the water for boating and water skiing, fishing, water explorations, and vacation cruises across the oceans and the seas of the world. When desired, some will even deep sea dive into the ocean for many reasons too vast to mention. Marine Biologist often spend much time in the water at the ocean's floor exploring plant life underneath the water.

Of course, we would never have been knowledgeable of the marine life had it not been for ma-

*Fire*

rine scientist who took upon themselves to dive in for a chance to explore the water content and the water consistency in the diverse bodies of water, which marine creatures actually resided on certain continents and so on..............

No matter how deep water is, as long as the conditions of the water are conducive to diver explorations, certain diving equipment can be used to submerge to the depths; whether a wet-suit, or a submersible vessel, to explore the substances and the mineral contents and the marine life of the water.

Unlike water; we are unable to dive into the midst of a burning fire to explore the qualities and the quantities of any molecular status to create the connubial consistency of the burning flames and the object consumed that make fire what it actually is. The unapproachable attributes of the fire assures that it stands out as the unmistakable natural element that it is. No one in their right mind would go diving into a burning fire expecting to come out of the fire yet alive!

No matter how hot fire is, or how cool the temperature of the blazing fire indeed is, there is never an opening that will allow anyone to step into the midst of the fire to check the consistency of the burning materials for the purpose of documentation; the creative assignment of fire won't allow for such manipulative waste, as the urgency of the fire is ever leading to the charred finish of everything burning in the flames; it's always rushing to totally consume the objects of its claim.

Time; in and of itself, it does not even allow for us to intellectually scrutinize the fiery exposition of the actual blaze as it is, when lit upon an object. It is the common reality that the temperature of any flame is too hot to physically manipulate to the point intent that we may be able to scientifically examine. Get into the fire if you choose to do so, just know that the fire will get onto you, and then it will get into you while on the way to the finish!

We are not totally sure as to whether the flames of the blaze are lit upon the object or as to whether the object itself is burning in the midst of the flames of fire, although we are able to witness the destructiveness of any object as result of the fire. In other words; does the objects burning in the fire create the ability for the fire to actually burn, or does the external oxidation give power and authority to the fire causing it to consume the objects caught in the path of the fire? Sometimes the answers to the questions are all of the above......................

The most powerful; most feared element known to us even to this very day and time in our history upon the face of the earth is fire. Fire mysteriously fell from heaven in a loaded flash of lightning that was powerful enough to ignite the entire surface of the ground with an immeasurable rate of speed. It is not known to us in the earth exactly where the lightning comes from or where the lightning returns, all we know is that it comes down with unrestricted power.

We still think that we have a monopoly on fire even though we have been unsuccessful at handling and containing fire on a consistent basis. We often fail to realize that the authoritative commander of fire is the same maker and the creator of the universe. If we are ever going to get a sense of control on fire, it would only have been realized because we had taken the control over God!

Everything that we know about fire is always after the fact of fire consuming upon any particular surface of something that has been burned. It's always the remnant fragments of the leftover charred residue that may in fact supply reasons that certain things might have ignited on fire, but it can't supply a reason for the fire itself! We know why things burn, but we don't understand the mystery of the flame that burned those things.

Sitting in a Sunday school class as a very young boy about 10-14 Years of age, when someone asked the question; "where did fire come from?" I can remember the Sunday school teacher giving us the scientific explanation that one day in a lightning storm, the lightning flashed very powerfully and struck a tree causing the tree to ignite on fire. However he never told us of who it might have been that told cavemen to even call it fire neither could they explain why the fire is hot!

They even went further to suggest that that was the initiation of cooking with fire, because the cavemen dropped their food in the fire, causing it to cook, whereas they ate the food now cooked by the fire, and have been doing it that way ever since. The statement is rather unintelligently lacking any substance to create a formidable explanation of the origin and the definition of fire itself and the now successful humanistic usage.

As it is, we of these latter generations of people feel as if we are the smartest people who had ever set foot on the earth. Who was there to explain to prehistoric cavemen that the fire would not do them any harm, especially since a fire of that magnitude was probably burning everything in sight? As a matter of the fact, who even told them to take cover and to find shelter away from the blaze of the fire? Scientist have traced fire back as far as to millions of years, however I have traced fire to the eternal existence of God! (Hebrews 12:29)

Think with me for a moment, who would tell those prehistoric individuals when to take their food away from the fire, realizing that it had been cooked sufficiently? Wouldn't you believe that they probably would have starved to death, seeing that they might have burned their food beyond the ability to eat it? How long would it have been before they discovered that they needed cooking utensils to cook their food keeping the food away from the blaze of the flames in the fire?

I have watched many documentary television events whereas men from the more modern civilization have traveled to remote villages to document the lifestyles of the far eastern tribes of Africa, Australia, the American Indians, China, West Indies, Japan, Malaysia, Central & South America and other secluded places on the planet earth. Over the years they have discovered methods of cooking their food, while it is yet a common practice to consume many of their foods raw!

However I have seen documented films whereas tribesmen took certain leaves from plants and the trees of the forest and wrapped their fish and meat in the leaves and placed it over and open fire to cook. Others have fashioned clay pots, and

*Fire*

have even molded metal pottery to be used as cooking utensils. As time has progressed onward, even those of the lesser civilized lifestyles, have developed a since of respectful handling of the fire, in that they have learned to keep away from the direct contact with the flames.

Even in this more intellectual era of living, we have a tendency to only prepare a meal when we are hungry; can't you imagine the dilemma of the lesser-intellegent people had their meal been lost to a fire? They hunted for their food according to projected scientific reports, whereas they did not even have the food storage compartments and refrigerators, so perhaps the only food that was being prepared would be the only meal at hand.

Had it been that those barbaric cave-dwellers that were illiterate of intellectual thought relative to the aid of fire to cook their food, come into contact with the flames, they would not have survived to report anything to us. Since fire has had the very same ability to consume everything, they would have been destroyed. Contrary to scientific historical suggestions, fire was a revelation to mankind; it was never a blind discovery that happened out of the blue! I thought it necessary to challenge the baseless ideas about fire and prehistoric man.

God; would had to have given mankind the operational guides to handle fire. Even today we go out of our way to teach small children about the destruction of playing with matches, in the hopes that they will learn the lessons taught and never fall victim to being the next fatality of the fire that burned down the house with them inside of it.

As children grow to be teenagers and young

adults they are still being taught lessons of fire safety, so that they will not burn down the house trying to cook a meal on the stove in the kitchen. Most men mature to believe that they are the neighborhood Bar-b-que authority; however, fire safety and cooking on the grill work hand in hand. As adults, we are still being admonished to maintain safety control over the fire in the grill.

It is rather intelligent to place boundaries around the place where fires are to be set. Fire is contained and controlled only for as long as we are in control of it and have set the proper boundaries so as to prevent the fire from moving outside of the intended containers. The very moment that fire gets out of control, it's off and running in any and every direction, whereas we only hope and pray that we are able to catch up to the blaze to extinguish it before too much damage has been done.

Stove manufacturers, place control settings on the knobs on the stove, not only to regulate the desired cook temperature, but to prevent the operators from opening the flames beyond user friendly controls, causing a fire in the kitchen. I know that you have gotten the message that I have been portraying to you in reference to the fact that fires are most apt to burn out of control, overstepping it's originally intended boundaries at even the slightest mishap or failure to keep a close watch.

### Ignited to Finish

The same fire that has been designed to be the greatest benefit to mankind has also proven to be the greatest destruction to us while living and in death, both in the natural and in the spirit. There

*Fire*

is not an animal, a man, an element or any particular substance on the face of this planet earth that is able to just naturally withstand fire without being totally consumed or destroyed.

Even in situations whereas a certain element is not totally consumed of the fire, that element is often disfigured, distorted, and thus damaged beyond the ability to be used. In its burned condition, the substance or element is of no usage, like as it was in its original state.

There is a phrase written into the elementary status of fire, which is the very same statement that Jesus uttered on the cross of Calvary; He said; "IT IS FINISHED!" The very moment a flame is purposefully ignited, the expectancy to complete the cause for haven needed a fire is believed to be successfully fulfilled. Fire in and of itself is not disappointing to the employed cause.

I wouldn't say that fire has evil intentions, but I will say that fire has a created purpose for which it is never found in failure to obeying its cause. We painfully regret and suffer immensely whenever we discover that fire had gotten to our stuff without our consent, because we know that fire never shows up to tease with our stuff! Only, we never intended for our things to have been met with the destruction of fire. The overpowering commanded purpose of fire is going to be fulfilled; fire will place all things in ruins without a doubt.

I have seen artificial fireplace substitutes, whereas the fireplace is fitted with artificial logs that are capable of producing flames, while a propane gas fire does indeed burn to create a source of heat. I don't believe that I have ever heard if there is even such a thing as a fire substitute! Never have I ever seen the need for the actual blaze of the fire abandoned, where the true blaze of the fire is needed, for a fire substitute, have you?

> For our God is a consuming fire.
> **Hebrews 12:29**

Some exhibitionist have been labled as the greater among their kind for their relentless abilities to walk on firery hot coals, they also know how to eat fire and the such; for which we are sure that these acts are only skilled illusions. We see men and animals jump through fiery hoops at the circus, and at other entertainment events; but you will never see any exhibitionist walk up and sit down in the midst of the fire.

Whenever we see these individuals handle the flames of the fire, we see them pass through the fire swiftly, for knowledge of the fact that the urgency of the blazing flames is moving about with extreme accuracy, and it will not fail to satisfy the swift ignition of anything that is caught in the midst of the flames.

Many ritualist and Occultist; use the leaping flames of fire for sadistic opportunities to chant, dancing around the flames, and sometimes even cutting themselves to carry out the ritualistic activities of their own sadistic practices. Massive barn fires are ignited to send up seasonal messages to the spirit world, signifying that they are in accordance to the spiritual affirmation needed to exist within the occultic reign.

In these civilized western hemispheric cultures of living, many of the younger people who have pledged to sorority and fraternity associations, many of them will brand themselves with hot branding irons in the fire at outdoor meetings, pledging their allegiance for life. They allow their physical bodies to be marred and marked permanently by the heat of the fire through the aid of an iron.

Such behavior has been the norm for African, Indian, Japanese, Chinese, Australian and many other historic tribes of people to brand them selves' for the purpose of tribal identification. Somebody among those of our ancestors discovered the fact that fire changes the origination of anything that it lights upon. Most likely this is also the common practical knowledge of the slave owners for which many of the slaves bore the branding marks of their slave owners on their bodies.

### Available, Plenteous, but yet Mysterious

The usage of the branding iron would serve the purpose of definitive control in the usage of the fire. Otherwise; the fire would prove to be as destructive as the lightning flash in the forest, lighting upon the grass and the trees in its striking path. It is plausible to believe that the need for a branding iron would be necessary through trial and error.

The filament in our light-bulbs produces what we should recognize as being captured fire within a glass quite similar to the lightning in the clouds. Once the switch has been turned on, the lightning flashes, only to a relentless consistency, to sustain the luminance produced from the fiery flash, thus providing an illuminated atmosphere much brighter for seeing and reading.

Even though fire remains a mystery in our grasp we realize just how much we really don't know about fire. Anywhere you look, and from every direction that you can get it, fire is available in one way or another, secular evil men have always tried to associate fire with everything evil. So; as a result of their misguided documentation, most people have failed to associate fire with God!

Somehow we in the natural apply the usage of fire for the purification of many different things. Firstly, the heat of the fire can usually kill bacteria and germs in the water thus rendering the water in a distilled purified state. Many germs and minerals have motion while in the midst of the water, for this reason alone the heat temperature seizes upon any elements and all particles in the water to subsequently cause the movement and the motion of the elements in the water to cease.

We know that even through biblical studies, that fire is used to heat the temperature of the crucible (melting pot) for melting gold, silver, and other precious metals for the purpose of separation of the impurities from the true elements. All that are the impurities will rest on the top frothing and bubbling in the pot obscuring what is the true gold and silver in the pot thus supplying what is now recognized as the dross, until the impurities are purged away.

Fire is used in the potter's kiln, to create a tempered furnace for the final finish of fine pottery so as to be prepared for consumer purchase and safe usage clean and clear of all impurities that would have been harmful to the touch upon coming into contact with anyone. Even in earlier times in

# Fire

this country of the USA, the sanitary departments used to burn the trash picked-up at the curb, it was ascertained that the fire would rid the society from all unnecessary germs and bacteria produced by the rotting trash.

The animal control centers used to also burn animal road kill, and diseased animals of all sorts. Now as of this present time I am not aware as to whether or not that practice is still in place. One thing's for sure; the mortuary and the funeral service providers are using crematories more often than at any time before than I can remember, as an alternative to burial in the ground. People are choosing fire as a means of death disposal, however, law enforcement and the F.B.I., have cited the increase of cremations as a means of destroying incriminating evidence relative to the decedent.

As mysterious as fire is to us, what I find more mysterious is the evidence that is produced and provided when the fire of the Holy Ghost rests upon any one of us. At this junction I neglect not to inform you that God is Fire! The Holy Ghost is not just spirit; but, "Fire!" Take the time to search the scripture and you will find that God has always been of fire, as fire has always been of God.

The burning bush in the book of Exodus, $2^{nd}$ chapter, is a clear picture of the fire that God truly is. The awesomeness of God yet present in His most gentle state and structure, burned urgently but yet eternally. I do believe that Moses could feel the temperature of the fire. Of which is the reality of the fact that he knew that the bush was indeed inflamed and burning furiously. But the most recognizable thing about the bush burning was the fact that the bush did not and would not burn up. The leaves and the branches of the bush just simply would not consume away with the flames, of which would normally be the expected results.

Had the burning bush been a natural thing of nature, time would have taken precedence on the burning flames and right there before Moses' eyes the bush would have consumed away into ashes, but because the occurrence was a spiritual phenomenon, the flames were of the eternal essence of God; therefore it had no time to burn in the since of burning that we are most accustomed of. There is absolutely no time in eternity, the natural bush of time could but only hold the fire of eternity in its bosom without becoming a casualty to the flames of the fire.

John testified that Jesus would come and baptize us with the Holy Ghost and Fire. Most people are stumped with the baptism of Fire? They can't seem to grasp the concept of being immersed into a bath of flames, but the eternal flame of the spirit is designed to come and sit largely in our bosoms. There is no time associated to the flames of the Holy Ghost; therefore we must understand that it comes to stay with us forever.

> And they were all filled with the Holy Ghost, and began to speak with other tongues, as the spirit gave them the utterance. **Acts 2:4**

The fire of the Holy Ghost is not that something that we can put on and then take it off after we have determined that we are satisfied to have had it on for a while. But, rather, it is a come on in that it is ordained of God to come on us to stay eternally. The Holy Ghost is in control of us, we are never in control of the Holy Ghost! The mighty burning fire of the Holy Ghost, rests upon us in the eternal essence of God; being the present entirety that God is and all that God ever was and ever will be!

The Holy Ghost is God in the fullness of the spirit and character of God! He is the completeness of His image and power, the actual movement of the realistic presence and power alive on the inside of us. The given presence of the Holy Ghost and Fire is the active flame of the spirit of God moving on the inside of everyone that has received the infilling of the spirit, as a result of having asked for it. The (HOLY GHOST); the whole experience of God!

### Burning Smart

Now that we know that God is a consuming fire; we need to understand that God in His own infinite wisdom, while He knows what things on the inside of us need to be burned up and removed from our beings, He is yet gentle enough not to totally consume our natural bodies. God is that flame of fire that we never have to ever worry that He will over step any burning boundaries. The God of all creation can never ever be out of order, nor out of bounds! He's too wise to ever make any kind of mistakes, thus He is never out of control.

He knows at all times just how much we all can bear, so we never have to worry that the fire of God is too much for us to handle. Some use the fear of not being able to handle fire as an excuse for not being filled with the fire of the Holy Ghost; of which is a grave error to the very necessary infilling of the spirit of God. God knows just where we need fire the most in our lives, meaning any sickness, disease, heartache, disappointments, letdowns, grief, loneliness, family crises, divorce, marriage, children, and etc......................

Of the greater mistakes made relative to the fire of the Holy Ghost is the assumption that the total association of the spiritual phenomenon was to have been kept within the four walls of the churches or at least to keep the need for the Holy Ghost within certain church denominational gatherings of Pentecostal believers. He; the spirit of truth is for every individual believer separately, but equally, to inform us of the ways of God, to show us the way to the truth and power of righteous and holy living in this present world.

Too many people are living out loud in sin and iniquity, confessing that they can't help themselves! Many people of the churches have allowed themselves to be weakened over time, as a result of giving way to the sin in their lives. The longer that sin stays on the inside of us without being bound and cast out of us, it get stronger and more powerful to control us, so as to ensure that we will never obey God.

For lack of teaching and proper instruction, many people have not come to the knowledge and the purpose of the baptism of fire; we are on our way upward once we have been saved, but, it takes the power of the fire to set us free! Alike a propelled rocket launched from it's launch pad, as it ascends upwards into the sky, there are certain

*Fire*

parts of the rocket that fall away allowing for the rocket to propel further into the sky. The parts which fall away simply burn up in the atmosphere as result of the fire attached to the soaring rocket.

As we desire to ascend into the heavenly spiritual realm with the spirit of God, we must understand that there are certain elements that are not at all acceptable for the spiritual reality of our change that can only fall away and be totally consumed so as to never be returned to us, by Satan or any other demon spirit. The fire consumes the weight and the sin that so easily attached itself to us as a result of having been living in a sinful atmosphere.

The fire of God rectifies and justifies our spirit and character, enabling us to be not only obedient to the spirit of the Lord, but it also helps us to identify with the spirit of God. The world will know for sure that we are God's when they hear us talk like Him, while we walk in holiness and purity of righteousness. They may never approve of the fact that we are God's children of a changed nature, and spirit; but they are able to know of it for real.

> And there appeared unto them cloven tongues like as of fire, and it sat upon each of them. **Acts 2:3**

It is always obvious that a person has not been baptized in the fire, because their mouths still speak like that of mere sinful men. Even in situations whereas they are standing in the pulpits of the churches, their carnal speech will give it away every time. It is not even until we have been baptized in the fire that we even find it necessary to separate ourselves from the wrong types of people, or at least from people that are wrong for us now that we are changed and accepted in the beloved. Be it friends, family, associates, co-workers, neighbors, and etc.....

The prophet Isaiah; in the year that his uncle; King Ussiah died (Isaiah 6:1), he saw the Lord and came under conviction that he had not been talking right. He said to the Lord; "I am a man of unclean lips, I even dwell among men of unclean lips." The angel of the Lord took one of the hot coals of fire from the altar and placed it on his lips. I believe that God was saying to Isaiah and to the rest of us, when in fact you cannot control your mouth, all you need is the fire! That spiritual fire cured Isaiah's problem of unclean speaking out of his mouth.

We remember the Prophet Elijah at Mt. Carmel; (I Kings 18:) while he encountered 450 prophets of Baal, and 450 prophets who sat at the table of Jezebel, whenever he brought them into question as to whether or not they would serve the Lord His God? It was by fire that the dilemma was solved as the fire fell from heaven as an answer from God signifying that he indeed is God. The fire licked up the water around the altar, upon the sacrifice of the altar, and consumed everything that was on the altar, and the actual altar itself!

The answers that we need are in the fire! The security that we need in today's churches is definitely in the fire! As leaders and as purported witnesses of God, we need to return to the fire of the Holy Ghost, and be lead by the purifying fire. So many instances of the fire written in the bible,

*Fire*

too many to write about myself, that will give a total understanding to the fire of God. The bible speaks for itself; take the time to read it!

We need fire in every way that we can think of and all of the ways that have not even been introduced to us as of yet in these latter generations. As things evolve and change in our civilization, many things are discarded and done away with as a necessity. We see this same behavior in and throughout the church communities, whereas many of the new and present leaders seem to have determined in their own minds that the baptism of fire is no longer necessary for the body of Christ.

If you have not realized that the mighty burning fire of the Holy Ghost makes the difference in the churches, then you have been blinded and are still lost in your own unbelief and sin! My urgency to the churches is to admonish every church and denominational affiliation to return to the fire now before it's too late, because those of us that don't come to the fire now and be baptized in the fire will be sent to the fire in eternity as a result of the judgment!

> And the devil that deceived them was cast into the lake of fire and brimstone, where the beast and the false prophet are, and shall be tormented day and night forever and ever. **Revelation 20:10**

Smart people think that they have discovered their own ways of dealing with Satan! It is totally outrageous to think that you can outsmart the devil, and handle demonic activity in the churches diplomatically so as to prevent disturbing the people in the pews. The people are already disturbed and demon possessed; they need to be delivered by the fire of the Holy Ghost.

The lack of Holy Ghost filled leadership is allowing the people to remain as demon possessed as they were when they first came into the church to be saved. Furthermore, the same unchanged people are taking over the more serious roles of administration in the churches. I say to you, do if you choose; but only know that the time is coming that you must answer to the fire;

> Every man's work shall be made manifest: for the day shall declare it, because it shall be revealed by fire; and the fire shall try every man's work of what sort it is. If any man's work abide which he hath built thereupon, he shall receive a reward. If any man's work shall be burned, he shall suffer loss: but he himself shall be saved; yet so as by fire. Know ye not that ye are the temple of God, and that the spirit of God dwelleth in you?
> **I Corinthians 3:13-16**

# Chapter Nine

# RIGHT NOW

*Therefore when he was gone out, Jesus said, Now is the son of man glorified, and God is glorified in him* . **St. John 13:31**
*And that, knowing the time, that now is high time to awake out of sleep : for now is our salvation nearer that when we first believed.* **Romans 13: 11**
*Now unto him that is able to do exceedingly abundantly above all that we can ask or think, according to the power that worketh in us* . **Ephesians 3: 20**
*Now faith is the substance of things hoped for, the evidence of things not seen* **Hebrews 11: 1**

Now unto him that is able to keep you from falling, and to present you faultless before the presence of his glory with exceeding joy. **Jude vs. #24**

Now: - *At the present time, often as opposed to in the past or in the future; at once or at this exact time. Used with statements of time to indicate that something has been happening for a particular length of time up to the present. Used to preface a remark, clarify a statement, get somebody's attention, or for emphasis*

Right:- *Correct -accurate, or consistent with the facts or general belief; proper -correct with regard to use, function, or operation; completely -used to emphasize how completely something happens, or that something is situated at, or moves or extends to, an extreme point; immediately -used to emphasize the immediacy with which something happens or should happen.*

*Right Now*

## Understanding Timing!

The word "NOW"; often looked upon as the oncoming time period for which a certain event is to happen being relative to a particular span in chronos, contemporary to the existing era; only a vast percentile of the general populas comprehend the expressed instance. It is also attributed to changes that have taken place, where the laws and the methods of living and doing things have been altered.

We need often to respect the evolving tide of motion and movement among the people of our society, whereas the necessary present ideas and manipulative skills of trade have matured to perform that which is more conducive to the present day speeds of travel and living, and the production of manufactured goods that enable newness; if not only for the present or {now-ness'}.

That which is often referred to as now, is respectively spoken to purposefully recognize the arrival of present opportunities. Now; also suggests the advantageous arousal in chronological succession to the destined order and epoch maturity of the thing next in line to come forth to produce that which had been conceiveable but held back in recognition to that which came before it.

The heightened maturation process whereas the requirements have been met to satisfy the fact of finding knowledge for a truth in a period of research, studies and learning, can often be suggestive to what is referred to as now. It is parallel to having crossed the finish line after the distance of the race, end to end; had been completed.

*Captured; Comprehensive; & Defined*

It is also comparable to the time of which we inhale after the reality of a life occurrence, which had been erected just in front of us hindering the possibilities for greater aspects of desired living; now that the hindrance is removed and our desire for living has come to fruition!

We should be able to distinguish the realistic span of now seeing that it is vastly evolving right before our eyes, from one actuality to the next without our consent. We may be in the midst of the storm now, but in just a little while when the storm passes over us, we may be in the rays of sunshine, or in the ruins of the storm's path of destruction. The one span of now has to yield in respect to the next.

Now; the period in time that we are acquiring information and data to get us through and over the hump, bespeaks of the process of preparation for any oncoming circumstance of life; now; we are presently prepared for whatever will confront our livelyhood; whenever?

Too often we are willing to associate the reality of Right Now to the similarity of the ongoing process of now, where we are ever learning, continuously going forth, and consistently digging while never finding anything, never learning anything, and never getting anywhere, or vice-versa. So many people are aspiring to become while they never accomplish the actuality of their desires to be!

Contrary to what many people have been led to believe, what we do in this life really does not give real true definition to who we are. As we begin to focus more clearly and up closely, we will

*Right Now*

also come to the knowledge of who we are at the presence, which should redirect our focus to the greater aspect of being somebody respectful and integral; rather than just doing something, just anything in this life.

For many people of today the idealistic reality is in the thought process of their own mind; they are convinced that if things don't get done now, well there's still time. A very great percentage of people are very sluggishly slothful whereas they have no aspect for immediately getting things done, dragging themselves through their daily routine, as if they could just fall off to sleep, right in the middle of their task.

The wind blows very powerfully, so often that it has the ability to change the appearance of the natural order of those things in the pathway of the actual wind gust. But what is actually more powerful than the gust of the wind blowing, is having the prior knowledge of what measures to take at the exact time when the wind will indeed blow. Knowing what action to take now or being skillful to take advantage of the wind blowing is a great benefit.

For an instance: an individual who will leap from a very high place of elevation for the purpose of hang gliding must know the right time to leap out to ride on the wind. Whenever there is no wind blowing, the glider stands a chance of crashing down to the ground, as a result of having no wind to support the wings of the glider.

On the other hand, many have suffered the tragedy of losing their lives as a result of a very strong gust of wind that had blown them off the course of their jump or glide. There have been reports of parachute jumper's landing in an alligator filled swamp, and others have even slammed into the sides of a mountain, crushing them to death. They simply had not properly judged the timing of the wind?

Perhaps they sought to take advantage of situations that would not be very advantageous for them? It only appears to us that they might have leaped before they actually looked! Or maybe they decided to look afterwards having jumped, for which it proved to be too late! In reality, we can never afford ourselves to do later on what should be done Right Now.

The individuals that would like to go windsailing out on the water, without giving careful considerations to the conditions of the weather, either one of two, or possibly three things might be the reality; The sailboat would only drift aimlessly without the strength of the wind to push the sailboat into the desired direction of the person that steers the boat.

We don't always understand why the water reacts to the wind like it does, but very unfavorable conditions are developed on the strength and power of the wind. There is such a thing as approaching the water at the wrong time according to the conditions of the wind blowing. A sailboat could be lost at sea, or simply destroyed and crushed by the angry waves of the sea.

Or lastly; the desiring sailor may have to concede to the conditions of the weather and sail on another day. Their plans would be disappointed as a result of the wrong timing. It is possible to know the timing of the wind. The problem is that most people are so arrogant, feeling they are in control of the world and the conditions that are natural to everyday living that they are lulled into focusing on back then, the last time, and they miss the need to see and to respect the conditions of this time; Right Now!

God does not always change the conditions that surround our lives, but He will change us for the conditions that we've been given to face, as we strive to live our lives. It is not that our daily conditions are deceptive to us as people of the earth; it is that we refuse to respect the conditions as they are even before we rise to answer the call to experience the blessing of a brand new day.

Many feel they have the power to change the normal conditions that place themselves in our path; We do not shape the conditions of our everyday lives; rather we are shaped in one way or another by the conditions of our lives. We have got to get with the conditions of our lives right now; finding ourselves in respect to the conditions which lend the drawing boards to strategize and maneuver our way around the situations, creating favorable circumstances for our now!

Wherever we find ourselves, at certain times of our lives, God is favorable to the crucial change concerning us in one way or another. There is really no such thing as being stuck in a situation whenever we get the revelation of what it really means to flow with the tide of Right Now. To be stuck bespeaks of the fact that you are bound by the past, whereas something or some situation has gotten a hold of you and will not let you go?

Right Now bespeaks of the forward progression of time and the immediate present motion of living for which we move forward every second of the day. It is impossible to be stuck when in all actuality we are in motion with God who is "RIGHT NOW"; moving forward towards the coming of the imminent return of Christ our Lord.

Look at your wrist watch, or the clock on your wall which may have a second hand moving every second, or perhaps your clock has LED function, whereas the dots between the numbers that represent the hour and the minutes on the clock are digitally flashing; every second hand move and every digital flash on the clock or on your wrist watch are the exact expression of the reality of Right Now; which is the movement of God!

Remember that God doesn't land on time; but rather time lands on and is in the forward progressive chase of the reality and the truthful existence of God. Therefore my friends, we are living in the Right Now existence with God. God said to Moses; I Am; that I Am...

The very statement of God's existence defies the dominance of time and or of the subversive binding hold of the past. We will always know and respect the fact that God is in control; not that God was in control, or that God will one day be in control; God is in control Right Now, forever!

Unless we come to the understanding of the reality of Right Now; we most likely will find ourselves left behind, and locked out of the reality of the move of God, as God won't stop the movement and the motion of time for any of us. Time is running on a mandated clock which has its own command to run until it runs out! Time in and of itself is not forever; Eternity is forever!

**We Have To Catch it On the Move**

The subtle fleeting reality of Right Now is so intangible for those who are asleep on their feet, who whist away their time being deceptively lulled to sleep on the apathetic stages of indifference with absolutely no accountability to one another, whereas people are determined to just live, let live, and die!

As I looked back over time past, I realized that many have gone on to the grave never having caught up to the never ceasing metronome ticking to the powerful cadence of always; Right Now!

My friend; Right Now; plays to the beat of a different drum, whereas every step that we take has got to be in rhythm to every progressive passing millisecond of the time, as the people of the Lord. Those who are out of step to the playing rhythmic cadence are also those who are out of the loop with the presence of God! God; never lag behind or drag along for the sake of those who are slothful and apathetic to the tides of change. So many people proclaim to be in the presence of God when in all actuality they are only desperately longing for the presence of the Lord.

It is a requirement for those of us who are determined to go all of the way with the Lord, to keep up in prayerful submission to the timing rhythmic movement of the spirit of the Lord. We have got to be able to hear the movement of the spirit as it passes through the atmospheres of our pathways of living, in which will attest to the fact that we are attuned, and attentive to the word and to the voice of the Lord.

Far too many people in the society of the churches feel that they are sharp enough to watch the movement of God; they feel that they are God watchers! They're convinced that they are swift enough to watch and see that which had only been ordained to be heard in the spirit but never seen until after the fact of the present movement. Although we have been commissioned to keep our eyes on the Lord, doing so only enables us to see when He chooses to show us as individuals, whatever He deems necessary to be seen.

No matter how spiritual you may have in fact become, there are some things that God is not going to show you! God; simply does not allow any of us to see everything that He does, for any reason! God is often too instantaneous and too quick for our eyes to behold or to set our focus upon to follow! God can do whatever He does so quickly, even right before our very eyes. We will have gone on for moments and even sometimes for hours and even days before realizing what had been done.

Right Now; instantaneously lands and moves too fast for us to take the controlling glances and stares that we are so accustomed to doing; that's right; Right Now is simultaneously landing and moving at instance of the the same movement that it takes to even be recognized in the reality of its existence. Therefore it behooves us to keep in step with the spirit of the Lord through the aid of the Holy Ghost, which enables us to hear and to feel the wind-like movement of the spirit as it blows past our individual beings.

I have learned; even as I keep on saying it; the greater things of the spirit of the Lord are caught and not taught! The catcher behind the batter at home-plate has to be watchfully aware and alert for the sake of the power of the batter swinging the bat at the fast ball approaching, and the speed of the pitch itself. His inability to focus and to remain alert just might mean winning scores for the opposing team, and it could mean a serious head injury.

Don't be deceived; the catcher has got to be listening as well as seeing the fast approach of the baseball. All of the skills of human intelligence have got to be working in an effort for the catcher to be as necessarily prolific as possible. And even when catchers are as skillfully aware as they are supposed to be at home plate, they must also be watchfully alert for the movement of the runners on bases that will attempt to steal the bases between the pitch.

So as we become catchers in the spirit of the Lord, we are alerted to never miss the hurling fast pace throws in the moments of Right Now! Some of our brothers and sisters are trying to quit on $1^{st}$, $2^{nd}$, and even $3^{rd}$ bases of living; in light of the fact that the enemy is trying to steal away right up under them to home base, trying to force a win against us even though the game had already been won from the start..........

As the moving reality of time passes our being, it should never pass without us being aware of the fact that it had just moved in succession to the given moments of glory which had just passed us. Of the greater mistakes that we as people make are the mistakes that are made during the times that we get excited! We allow excitement to steal the oncoming moment of time from us because we lose focus on ourselves in the shock and awe of an excited moment.

In excitement we hold on to the moment passed whereas we never even give reverence to each moment that is passing right up under us, Right Now! We become so ecstatic at what happened that we purposefully fail to realize that moments are ticking away, whereas in many instances it is actually time that is ticking away.

### Now That We are Here; Right Now; Is!

The beauty of the reality of Right Now is that it is right here! That's right; you're sitting, standing, you may be lying down in it, someone is even asleep in the midst of it; Right Now! You don't have to go anywhere to look for it, just know that it's wherever you go, wherever you are, and it is wherever you will ever be; whenever and every time that you are there! Right Now; is everywhere and all of the time!

There is no escaping the reality of Right Now, and don't worry about being accused of being selfish because of your determination to adhere to the present urgency and focus on Right Now. Many people will prefer that you live in the past, as well as a great number of people who think that they are innovative and smart they will want to keep you living in respect of the possibility of the coming future here in the earth.

Most people either want to live behind, or they think that they can successfully live ahead of the present time. Here is what I mean: always speaking in reference to the way things used to be back in the day; or always talking in reference to how glad they will be when things change, which is relative to the futuristic advancement of the present time of which we are living.

In either case scenario, they are overlooking the actual placement of where it is that they are Right Now in the very moments of their realistic existence, whether it is intentional or simply overtly an oversight in ignorance! Although some make every effort to be as subtle as possible to behave in this manner, careful not to be offensive to the average person, they're still at a disadvantage to take hold of their present state.

You may often be referred to as being either unmovable or overly affixed to your reality for having a Right Now grasp on living, simply for the fact that people are determined to suggest that we keep it moving when in fact things that are associative to us are in need of the attentiveness that would put the finishing touch to them for our benefit. Too often the mindset to just keep it moving, breeds the attitude of slothful apathy to leave things undone and unfinished.

In elementary school back in the fifth grade, I remember a poem that I was given to recite for a school program written by James Weldon Johnson, titled; "Do It Now!"

The allotted time to get things done is moving right out from beneath us quicker than we realize and faster than we really want it to. Smart people feel that we should live reaching forth to all of the newly awarded opportunities of living, but, all while never having had the very necessary grasp or a grip on the power and the reality of Right Now. Is it really wise to pass present opportunities for future opportunities?

It is common to hear people speak in reference to letting go of things and moving onward in life; however most people have never realized the fact that Right Now is what is actually moving on forward having released its grip on things among the living at each momentous tick of the clock, faster most times than we are often aware of!

Right Now; never holds on to back then; it used to be; nor, it was at one time back in history; it is too swift and essential for the purpose of forward progression to be tied or anchored to anything that would hinder its fleeting command to enhouse the present engagement of motion.

Now that we have come to this comprehensive stand of reasoning to the relativity of "Right Now"; let's not resolve to disregard the seriousness of the topic of discussion, simply for the sake of being complacent and resistant to the need to change in respect to the way that we view the reality of living as if time is at our disposal and on our side. Time doesn't stop to hold friendly conversations with anyone, or pause to share intimate moments of memorable essence.

If all of the clocks should cease to operate and to properly keep up with the movement of time; we would soon discover that time itself would have continued to progress in movement towards the imminent coming of the Lord to return to receive the church out of this world. The forward motion of time will never stop simply because the time keeping mechanisms had ceased to properly function correctly reporting the accurate hour, minute, and second of the time.

The days of the week, one after the other, continue to move forward in progression opening and closing, in and out of the accurate timing in succession to the chronological order of forward progression as we know of it since before we even came to the earth ourselves to live and realistically validate the present generation that we have been born to live and to fulfill our predestined purpose.

We are witnesses to the ongoing scheduled re-occurrence of having the sun to rise in the east and to set in the west, realizing the oncoming breaking forth of the daylight, and the submergence of the earth's atmospheric splendor and visage blanketed beneath the evening shade and dark shadow of the expected but, appointed nightfall.

Whether indoors or outside in the open air, we are witnesses to the present shades of Right Now, as it passes at each moment of the day, no matter what hour. Should we stand in direct exposure to the rays of the sunlight, and even until the sun has completely set for the evening, we would be able to see the casting of the individual shadow on the surface of the ground in that it moves at a certain percentage with the movement of the hourly rate of time on the clock.

At each hour, the shadow of everything in direct exposure to the sunlight moves clockwise in forward motion to the Right Now progression of the time. It is amazing that not even a shadow casted on the ground does not stand still during the passing of the time of Right Now! As Right Now;

moves so does everything else!

As a boy I used to go to the corner store to buy a package of candy called "Now-Laters." The candy manufacturers were rather brilliant in their design of this particular package of candy, in that they packaged each individual piece of fruity candy, some for now and some for later. I would eat a few pieces of the candy immediately, share a piece or two if I so desired, and eat the rest of the candy later. Sometimes even days later!

Since the years have passed, and I have matured to adulthood as a grown man, it has been revealed to me just how much like the package of Now-Laters salvation really is. As long as I have possession of the wrapped candy, I can enjoy some for now and then of course some for later. As long as I purposefully remain connected to the true vine, salvation will keep me safe now, and then of course it will keep me safe later on.

Salvation is good now; Right Now; and later on it will be still good again Right Now. So my now good, will be still my now good, later on; it will be now-later on, Right Now!

# Conclusion

## MY FINAL SAY ON THIS MATTER:

Captured; Comprehensive; & Defined

My intentions are to influence you to live on purpose in everything to which you submerge yourself to absorb and all that you will ascend to that is applicable for elevated platforms of living with extreme motivations from deep down within you for having a knowledgeable assurance of understanding relative to the purpose in which you are even alive. I n these most crucial times of our lives, we need to know who God is, who we are, what we are doing, where we are going, what we are truly achieving, and that we are destined not just for greatness but for God in Heaven as our greatest achievement!

Wouldn't you agree that it is absolutely ludicrous to continue meandering in winding circles going around the same mountain having no inclination for real success, encircling and entrapped without a clue pertaining to how to get off of that ride to nowhere? So many people of the churches are easily influenced by detractors and enemies of the faith of God in Christ Jesus; simply for the reason of their own blind searches, and incomprehensible information they have received which eliminated firm foundational platforms to rest their faith upon.

Having the mind of Christ and living life according to the word of God in total obedience with a determination to please the Lord is God's will and plan for us; in contrast to living by carnal secular influences and the willful disregard to the obedience of the word of God from other people, even though they are members of the local church; are two totally different things! Many unbelievers who are members of the local churches dangerously use the power of their negative influence to persuade and to dissuade others away from believing God and the Holy Bible. And then again; there you have the overzealous groups of believers who are determine to be right, even though it separates the body of Christ and allow for beliefs of the word of God to be segregated and foul.

    We need desperately to re-explore what is referred to as "faith based agendas;" programs that only generate financial influxes but have nothing to do with the increase of faith in God! People who long since before now had begun to entertain the idea of leaving God and the church, have begun to put those thoughts into action, whereas the reports are that the Christian churches are dwindling away.

    There is really no way for the Christian church to dwindle away, as the power of the church is not in the hands of man but Christ. Those; who so easily fall away from the church were never in the church from the perspective of having had their souls saved from sin and their hearts changed to the point that they had sold out to living holy and separated from the influence of this present worldly society. I'm referring to people who prefer the Nightclub atmosphere in the churches rather than to be in the presence of the Lord. Or they simply prefer churches that do a lot of religious stuff with no real meaningful penetration of their own spirits.

    In a very paralleled essence in dissimilarity, most people are really not living as much as they are merely existing, unfulfilled in the survivor mode accepting life as it comes day in and day out! They are always on the defensive having no answers to the difficult questions in their lives, not knowing where to go to find the answers either. More commonly in certain areas of society opportunities, career advancements are omitted on purpose for fear of the unknown, being insecure of the ability to succeed, or to fit in on a new platform of living with wealthier people?

    People don't fear poverty and lack in the least, as they accept it every day! But, however, lacking methodical comprehension they are seriously unprepared for prosperity and riches not actually knowing how to handle real money and financial decisions to make wise investments! Just remember how often it's been that we heard through the media that someone had won the lottery, winning millions of dollars, only to hear soon afterwards that they had also gone broke again!

Understand me; money is not what makes any person a fool concerning finances; only money will expose the foolish intentional planning to mishandle a lot of money that had already been festering on the inside of you for years waiting on the right opportunity to leap out of you! Having money won't make you a proud arrogant individual, but if you allow money to puff your head up to believe that you are someone that you are not it will alleviate any reasonable behavior for which you had kept pride and arrogance under the cover of the blood of Jesus hidden away from public indecency as a true believer.

Precautions are rarely considered in relation to the bends and the curves that will take us so unsuspectingly along the roadways of life as we travel along; I say often that people are caught trying to build storm shelters in the middle of the storms! In times of trouble, they have no place to go; and neither have they spent the necessary time in prayer to sustain them. They're doing whatever it takes to get by whether they understand the methods that they use to get where they are going or not. The very people that are powerless, it appears often; they are the very people that have powerful tendency to take the control of their lives and others but they don't realize it, or they refuse to embrace it!

Living does matter! What we do and say and how we manifest the choices that we have been given by God to choose from in this life, does make a difference. It's left up to us to captivate the understanding that we need to motivate ourselves to be at the very top of our game; (if you will allow me to say it like that?). We have meaning that is not just to be pulled down out of a cloud in the sky or from outer space. Power must be realized and determined of the sort and the source from which it flows to us, whether it is from God or not; prior to any attempt to be successfully influential to effect change for ourselves or for anyone else.

We are naturally apprehensive about sheltering ourselves under the protection of our living conditions being vigilant and adamant of never spending the greater percentage of our time loitering in the cemetery among the tombs where no activities of living exist, of course with the exception of when the living are burying the dead. Even those who are homeless living on the streets, at daybreak when the sun rises on the face of the earth, they rise to their feet and begin to reposition themselves about the town; although they are often frowned upon and regarded as nonproductive to society, most still show desires for living; they would like to do better than they are doing. It's the normal behavior of people everywhere, even of them that are incarcerated, to wake up from sleeping and prepare themselves to move about their planned agenda in the run of each day, unless they are in the lesser percentage of those who attempt to sleep all day long.

I am motivated to enlighten you of the fact that too many people are doing things and going to places without a true clue to what it is that they are doing, and are lost in definition of where they are on a daily basis! We will all at times make the mistakes of believing that just because people are standing right in the middle of situations and places, that they know exactly where they are in true definition. We have developed the bad habit from our youth up of giving everybody the benefit of the doubt; in all actuality we might better serve the needs for one another should we take it for granted that others know until we ask and are made aware that they do know for sure!

We even employ people to repair and to remodel

certain things for us only to discover that they know only a fraction of the information that would really meet the criteria to attest that they are trained and qualified to do the job.

So; where we go from here to really make us complete, entirely with integrity is to reassume the search for the information that will increases our capacity to launch forward as productive individuals; we need to be reinvigorated to take on the chase that promises to award us the respectable status of our desired explore; and finally we need to rekindle and to stir the motivations to be counted among the elitist of our society remembering that we are the head and not the tale; above only and not beneath, as children of faith in Christ. (Deut. 28:)

It is of the most importance to center a microscopic focus upon yourself; as a matter of the fact it is paramount to know you beyond the shadow of a doubt, and to know that you have taken the precautions necessary to make it in this life. Nothing in this life is for free, as you will seldom if hardly you will ever find anyone that is giving away that that you will need for you and for your family to manage from day to day.

Not only that; but, you should find it indispensable within yourself to be able to stand on your own, not having to depend upon someone else to support you, or to depend upon their knowledge to get you through life. There is a since of self-worth to be established on the inside of ourselves which only comes from pursuing those things which grant us the mental fortitude and the stability to create balance as we progress in life.

The Lord must lead us for sure and we must be willing to follow the Lord as He leads us, but being able to comprehensively follow the Lord not having to be led by someone else is a blessing indescribable. Being proud of others doesn't necessarily hold a candle light to the pride that one will have in themselves when they will have accomplished and acquired knowledge and skill to walk in their own assigned pathway of living out their own destiny.

As a minster of the gospel, I know that there are a lot of things that people in general do not understand, or they just don't take the time to find the understanding. So, therefore being a lover of the people of the Lord, I find it necessary to lend a helping hand to show someone the way enabling them to stay with the Lord, having answers to their questions and sufficient reasons to supply answers for the questions of others that will ask of them a reason of their hope.

### Captured; the Chase?

Listen to me when I say to you that absolutely nothing can be captured that has never been sought after, hunted, or neither pursued with the serious intentions to have the possession and the ownership of the thing or the item/element of knowledge; for the ultimate purpose of intellectually enhancing oneself to stand on the heightened plateau of learning and the sanctity of matured rationalization for living.

Regardless of the purpose for which a thing, a person, or an element of knowledge has been pursued, the possession could never have been possible had the desire to go after the thing to conquer it been put into action, as is the manner of a true captivator. Many things in this life will have a tendency to flee our possession alike a fugitive who flee the capture of the U.S. Marshall's Task Force. It may appear that things are fleeing and running with serious intentions to escape being captured alike a deer fleeing the sights of the hunter's rifle. So; it behooves us to get after it with very aggressive motivations and adamant intentions.

Often in the churches, lots of information has been given to people who never wanted the knowledge in the first place, so the knowledge is rejected and cast aside as insignificant. The very purpose of knowing has never been for the purpose of applicable structure for living. This is so mainly because many people of the churches and of other societal associations and affiliations are often operating as explorers in search of whatever there is that could be found through happenstance discovery by chance. They are not people in pursuit of those things of which they most desire that have been identified and reckoned to be a possession of their own.

In all honesty, people are consistently pursuing knowledge and all knowledgeable acquisitions, but only for the purpose of stock piling information on the storage shelves of their minds as if to ready themselves with the ammunition to intellectually battle with all that would be posed as opponents to their order of thinking and applied learning, as well as posturing themselves competitively for any platform debates to intellectually spar with their like constituents.

Many have gotten the memo that there is information available just waiting to be mentally consumed. Those who care about education and knowledge are aware of the extensive lines to register and to apply for classes on the college campus during registration; people are waiting in lines by the thousands across the country to apply for the classroom courses of their chosen fields of study. However, in life there are people standing in imaginary lines, just to hear and learn information to which perhaps they have never learned before. But it is often information that is pointless and doesn't even apply to the lifestyle that they are living.

At each opportunity to take advantage of the knowledge buffet transversely spread across the globe, many have mentally gorged themselves almost to the point of an overload mental blowout; they have come to understand that learning reveals the reality of the vast platitude of information available for mind consumption only should they never desire to put the knowledge into action! Knowledge itself, is taken simply just because it's there. Knowledge taken does not necessarily bespeak of the fact that the knowledge has been reasonably figured out and successfully placed with each step taken to make choices daily.

A greater percentage of elevated thinkers are so stuck at the level of mentally perceiving; they are consistently attempting to figure everything out in their own minds, almost never moving to the place and point of actually creating smoother platforms of living for themselves as a result of the knowledge that they had acquired. Those who allow themselves to be stuck in perception are also often found perusing the thoughts of others concerning themselves relative to what is being said about them.

This particular mindset is often the reason that many never capture the knowledge and the other accomplishments that they are pursuing in life. The ability to focus and to stay focused is definitely compromised when a person has become preoccupied with the thoughts and action of others. It's necessary that we as the pursuers be sternly focused in fact to be sure that the things to which we chase are the exact things that we take possession of. Whatever we are going after in life is never really to be the concerns of others.

How embarrassing is it to take the captured things out of the bag, figuratively speaking; only to realize that the thing taken is not even what you were chasing? What a waist! You laid hands on the wrong thing for any number of reasons. Now you find yourself in explanation to others as to how you spent all of your time going after the wrong thing, when all along it looked like the exact thing that you were determined to have.

Before you ever start your chase, be assured of just what it is that you are actually in pursuit of. You see it can be your due season, but it may not be the exact time in your season to take the possession of your harvest! Plan the strategies of your pursuit, alike the farmer who plant seeds for a specific crop to insure an ultimately intended harvest just at the right time in the due season. Knowing what it is that we want should work hand in hand with how we plan the pursuit of what it is that we actually intend to capture.

The capture, alike salvation and being saved from sin is the initial part of it all and the simplest to acquire. It's that thing that you just go ahead and do. You never spend the balance of time in pursuit of salvation; you just receive salvation through faith and repentance. If you can believe the work of Christ on the cross of Calvary, and receive that He did it all just for you, there is nothing else for you to do but to receive it through repentance of your sins, in doing so you will have captured what had initially been given to you. At this point you have got to be willing, as well as capable of thoroughly examining what you have taken possession of, for the purpose of knowing what it is that you have now. You've done the easiest part of having your possession, which was captivating and claiming it as your own.

Life is just too short for us to acquire a lot of things for no purpose at all; for example: becoming hoarders of things and knowledge just because we could have the things. Stuff has a tendency to weigh us down and even to slow us down hindering us on our journey through this life that we have been given to live. Whatever we have should bring meaning with it, and be purposeful to remain with us as we move forward in life, otherwise we should not be hesitant to throw things overboard should it be discovered that certain things have been holding us back from reaching our goals.

## Comprehensive; Understand it?

What does it mean; what is the purpose; what is the function; what are the benefits; how does it apply to our lives? Do you have the answers? It is to you that it matters the very most, not the understanding of anyone else that should make the difference to you unless you are the teaching instructor in need of knowing that your students are learning.

I have never climbed a coconut tree, but I have observed that it is a skillful journey making the way up the tall tree for the coconuts atop of the tree. Once the journey has been made up and back down the tree with the possession of the coconut, the next step is to crack it open! That's right, to get the hard shell of the coconut opened should be the very next business at hand, else the journey was all for nothing, in terms of personal consumption. Both the milk and the meat of the coconut are beneficial for food consumption, therefore I could not see taking the coconuts just for the purpose of ridding the tree of the coconuts just to prove to anyone that you could scale the tree.

I can't eat any seafood or fish with the exception of Tuna salad well prepared, and that's not that often. So it doesn't make since to me to go fishing and deep sea diving for the purpose of catching sea animals for the benefit of food consumption knowing that I could never partake of those items for food. Many people even go on hunting expeditions for wild game to which they have no appetite for. They shoot and kill game animals just for the sport of it all and take it home to give it away; or if they can get away with it, the game animals are just left out in the field for other predators to consume.

In other words it's a waste of time and energy to go after things that we really don't desire for ourselves relative to the fact that there is a benefit in having those things in the first place. As nothing from nothing, leaves nothing; I have also come to understand and to realize that nothing; means nothing! Just as there are certain animals in the wild that supply absolutely no benefit to us as human beings, there are also certain fish and aquatic animals in the ocean and the sea that are likewise of no benefit for human consumption; as a result those certain animals are left in their places to balance out the eco-system of the water world.

So tell me what are you working with, where is it that you are working from, and then tell me why is it that you are working at all? We must never make the mistake of forgetting that God, Himself; He makes no mistakes! To qualify that statement, let me remind you of the fact that God is still the God of measure. Remember the story of how it was that the master gave to one servant ten talents, to another he gave five, and to the other he gave him only one? With little to almost no regards to what they each did with their gifts, let's respect the fact that the gifts were given to each of them according to their own measured capacity to receive.

God knows what we are starting out with as we begin to work, so He deals with us according to our measures. The scripture teaches us that every man has been dealt the measure of faith; therefore God knows where to start with us according to our measures. It is often the fact that those who start out with more often end up with more when they have been wise and prudent in their dealings. That which has indeed been determined as more, that an individual might have, is going to be revealed by what it is that they have gone after in their drive to acquire while searching. For some it has been wisdom while others are in search of having all of the stuff that they can find and handle.

Wisdom will lend the control strategies to manipulate and to maneuver all of the stuff and the things that we acquire in life. There is a grave difference in the determinate status distinction of those of us whenever we are filled with hearty desires to want and when we are indeed filled with wise dominion to be in control of ourselves and our stuff never allowing things to have dominance over us, to which God knows about every one of us individually. Some things in life we are just going to have regardless, but the difference will be in knowing how to handle the things that we have and what to do with them.

Only wisdom has the power to prevent things from being erected as the establishing factors that make us who and what we are. Without wisdom we allow things to identify us, as if to be the defining factors of our lives. Perhaps, it may be the car that we drive, or the house that we live in, or the corporation, of which we are employed, or even the church where we are members or pastor, or finally the school in which we attended?

Whatever the case, those things only have the power to tell what it is that we have done or the places where we find ourselves on a daily basis, or maybe even weekly, but it does not have the power to truly define who we are. We do know that a lot people attend the church who are not at all surrendered sanctified Christians washed in the blood of Jesus Christ. Just as people walk through the shopping malls all day long and never purchase a thing as it was never their intentions to do so in the beginning.

What do you understand about the things that you have, and what do you really know about the places that you go, or what is it that you have been made aware of concerning the positions that you hold? You may indeed know that you have authority, but for what reason has the authority been given to you? Is your authority detrimental to you or is it beneficial to the people of God? Do you really know?

Just because we may already have a certain thing for our possession, it doesn't mean that those things are really good for our benefit! Wise comprehension teaches us to relinquish some things from our possession, as they are proven to be no good for us, or for anybody who come into contact with us. We learn the true disdain of greed through understanding and fortified comprehension. We know not to try and catch more fish than our boats are able to carry back to the shore, else our boats will sink into the water being over-weighted, whereas we may also even be drowned. It's also to the likeness of knowing which fish are not good for human consumption, so we automatically throw them back into the water.

However, better comprehensive knowledge enables us to understand why those inedible, poisonous fish are in the water to begin with and what their purpose is to the aquatic life cycle. Certain particular fish devour live bacteria and other parasites that are contaminable to the flesh of the fish while in the water; should the fish be infected or contaminated it would definitely be harmful to us should we ingest them into our digestive system. God in His own infinite wisdom, He has placed certain fish in the water to solve that problem for us before ever catching the fish out of the water to be eaten.

Understanding; in my own opinion; is one of the greatest accomplishments that anyone can have? The reason that Jesus used parables in the scripture was for the sake of enabling those whom He taught to come to a clearer understanding. Relativism is of the greatest tools of comprehending things in this life; it helps us to connect the dots, as in a game with dominoes; also, alike connecting the shapely configured pieces of a jig-saw puzzle. The pieces fit somewhere in the puzzle but we have to distinguish the relative shapes and apply the flatted platform conjoining shapes of the fittings on the surface of the completed picture of the puzzle.

## Defined; I've got it now!

    Maybe I think too deeply at times; however, I often think to myself, that people can't see clearly who wear very dark tinted eye-ware over their eyes, even in the night or in the darkest of most atmospheres? When looking through dark glasses, everything on the opposite side of the eyeware is slightly darkened and altered in its hue. The actual colors of the images that we view are optically skewed and altered whereas they can't be seen clearly as they really are. Even the whiter, brighter colors are visibly declined to deeper shades of color as long as there is a darkened shade skewing the image.

    Sun shades are a great benefit to the eyes to protect the eyes from the danger of the sun u.v. rays, and the extreme sunlight at high noon when the light of day is the brightest. But I don't get it when I see people wearing sun shades in the house or in church, or just simply indoors where the sun is not in dominance of the interior atmosphere. See there has to be a reason for all that we will ever do in this life; it's called purpose!

    In all that has been written in this particular literary work, it has been penned for the purpose of igniting the minds to recognize and to realize individual purpose of people, places, and things. It is even necessary to know the purpose of the things that are relative to our everyday living, especially those things that we normally take for granted. Most people have a least a minimal understanding as to why God created the dirt on the ground; but most people don't have a clue as to the reason that there are rocks in the dirt, and even very large rocks beneath the surface of the ground? We just know that the rocks are there.

We're familiar with rocks from the standpoint of picking them up to throw them for any number of reasons? We also recognize that rocks are solid and non-porous whereas no water is allowed to pass through the rocks alike the dirt and sand which becomes thick and slimy creating what we know of as mud when water has been applied to it. Water has an effect on the looseness of the dirt that it can never have on the solidarity of a rock?

It is very simple to walk out of dry dirt having only a dusty dulling residue on our feet or shoes; however, should we walk through the wet mud we will drag the mud all over every other surface that we walk on as result of the mud that has attached itself to our feet and our shoes soiling them whereas they are in need of being cleansed from the residue of the slimy sludge. Water saturation changes the effectiveness of the dirt or sand causing it to act and to even react differently under the wet conditions.

See; here is the plight of the churches at large; most of the people of the churches are dragging the mud of their own sifted religious views about Christ, and the salvation of humanity resulting from the shed blood of Jesus on the cross of Calvary which has been diminished to the consistency of the sand all over the face of the planet, thus obscuring solid foundations of faith in God. The addition of the water to the sand to make mud, which of itself, the water is indicative in meaning to that of the more common troubles of the times of our society's present existence.

Rather than passing the rock around the world, the churches are dragging the theological mud of religion all around to the churches and the surrounding communities, wherever they can get it in. So, as a result, the people are soggy and soiled as a result of the mud, rather than being founded upon firm foundations as result of the solidarity of the rock of ages. Once the moisture has been evaporated from the wet mud the dirt consistency come together to form very hard crackling type surfaces which can never be compared to the hard surfaces of the rock, or concrete.

In this life we have trials and some troubles, for which the rock of Jesus offer solutions and shelter from the destruction of the onslaught of the devastating mudslide coming down the hillside against us as we journey upwards towards the presence of the Lord. We never expected trouble in the churches whenever we came to the Lord to be saved, but to our surprise we were broad-sided by the unforeseen steamroller magnitude of trouble crushing everything in its path, whereas we discovered that nothing else offered a suitable solution to the problems but Christ!

The church use to sing a song that said; "be very sure that your anchor holds and grips that solid rock! That rock is Jesus, He's the only one!" In times like these very unstable situational circumstances, we need a solid firm foundation. Things are like that of quick sand; I have the understanding that quicksand is simply sand consistency which has taken on all of the water that it can take, whereas the sand doesn't come together like that of the dirt to make mud. However, the water eliminates the ability of the sand to stay together at the very least. Too much water!

The world is truly in trouble; especially now that people are more determined to live without the influence of the word of God and the spirit. They have not realized that they have destroyed their real solutions to the problems that they are having, only to create more problems attempting to fix things on their own. Even whenever we know how to fix certain things, it doesn't prevent those certain things from breaking down. It is even more grievous to deal with broken things to which we have no clue as pertaining to what broke them down, having no knowledge to restore them to their original condition, in working order.

There are some things in this life that we ought to know else when things go wrong, as it has been doing as of late at alarming rates, we are rendered incapable of a reasonable fix. For too long without the aid of the Lord to help us to get a handle on things, the things that we need to get handled spiral out of control in that they get out of our reach and beyond our scope of knowledge to bring things back into a foreseeable range of scrutiny so as to be able to repair that which is indeed broken.

See, I've got it now!

I need the Lord; not just the help of the Lord, but I need the presence of the Lord daily alive in me living through me to aid me in all of my daily affairs. Even the more common things that I may be able to handle on my own, I invite the wisdom of the Lord to help me not to make a mess of those things as well. I am dependent upon the Lord, and it doesn't matter who disagrees with me on this;

# God; is my, everything; I can't go wrong with Him!

www.ingramcontent.com/pod-product-compliance
Lightning Source LLC
Chambersburg PA
CBHW051432290426
44109CB00016B/1522